New World, Known World

New World, Known World

—⁓—

Shaping Knowledge in
Early Anglo-American Writing

David Read

UNIVERSITY OF MISSOURI PRESS

COLUMBIA AND LONDON

Library of Congress Cataloging-in-Publication Data

Read, David, 1956–
   New world, known world : shaping knowledge in early
Anglo-American writing / David Read.
        p. cm.
   Summary: "Examines the works of four writers from the
early period of English colonization: John Smith's Generall
Historie of Virginia, William Bradford's Of Plymouth Planta-
tion, Thomas Morton's New English Canaan, and Roger
Williams's A Key into the Language of America (in conjunc-
tion with The Bloudy Tenent of Persecution)"—Provided
by publisher.
   Includes bibliographical references and index.
   ISBN-13: 978-0-8262-1600-7
   ISBN-10: 0-8262-1600-5
   1. United States—History—Colonial period, ca. 1600–1775—
Sources. 2. United States—History—Colonial period, ca.
1600–1775—Historiography. 3. Great Britain—Colonies—
America—History—Sources. 4. Great Britain—Colonies—
America—Historiography. 5. Smith, John, 1580–1631. Generall historie of Virginia, New England, and the Summer Isles.
6. Williams, Roger, 1604?–1683. Key into the language of
America. 7. Bradford, William, 1590–1657. History of Plymouth Plantation. 8. Morton, Thomas, 1575–1646. New
English Canaan. 9. American literature—Colonial period,
ca. 1600–1775—History and criticism. I. Title.
   E191.R43 2005
   973.2—dc22

                                    2005015403

♾ This paper meets the requirements of the
American National Standard for Permanence of Paper
for Printed Library Materials, Z39.48, 1984.

Designer: Kristie Lee
Typesetter: Crane Composition, Inc.
Printer and binder: Thomson-Shore, Inc.
Typefaces: Dante and Chesterfield Antique

In memory of John Malcolm Wallace,
rara avis

Contents

—ɯ—

Acknowledgments

—⚬—

First I want to thank Tom Quirk for his help, and I mean *help* in the broadest sense. He would likely deny that he has ever been of assistance to anybody, but many will think otherwise. I also am grateful to Janel Mueller and Janice Knight, who were generous enough to provide early outlets for the work of a wholly self-taught and somewhat wet-behind-the-ears early Americanist, and to Trish Roberts-Miller, Bill Kerwin, Mo Lee, Frances Dickey, Pat Okker, and Noah Heringman for reading and commenting on different parts of the project. I thank the presses of the University of Chicago and the University of North Carolina for permitting me to make use in Chapters 1 and 2 of work that initially appeared in article form in, respectively, *Modern Philology* and *Early American Literature*. Chapter 4 is the product of a much-appreciated research leave funded by the University of Missouri Research Board. My appreciation goes as well to the anonymous readers at the University of Missouri Press for their astute and constructive suggestions about improving the manuscript; I want them to know that I have tried! That I treasure the constant support of my wife, Sarah, and daughters, Anna and Molly, goes without saying, but I will say it anyway.

This book is dedicated to the memory of one of my professors in graduate school at the University of Chicago, John Wallace, who, like the writers I am studying here, came from England to North America to make a career. At one point in my doctoral program he was pressed into writing a qualifying examination for me on the topic of the literature of travel and exploration, and he confided to me with a chuckle that he had never written a test on a topic about which he knew so little. If he were still among the living, he might not know what to make of my latest transatlantic excursion, but I am fairly sure he would tell me that at least (and at last) I was working in the right century. His idea of paradise was the Wooded Island in Jackson Park during the migratory season, and I hope that in some fashion he is still there, checking off the remaining North American birds on his life list—perhaps even a western tanager like the unmistakable male that I saw in a hedge on Ellis Avenue one autumn morning and that my teacher was thrilled to know had passed by chance through his neighborhood, though he merely heard about it from me and never saw it himself.

A version of Chapter 1 appeared earlier as "Colonialism and Coherence: The Case of Captain John Smith's *Generall Historie of Virginia*," in *Modern Philology*, volume 91, copyright © 1994 by the University of Chicago. All rights reserved.

A version of Chapter 2 appeared earlier as "Silent Partners: Historical Representation in William Bradford's *Of Plymouth Plantation*," in *Early American Literature*, volume 33, copyright © 1998 by the Department of English at the University of North Carolina. Used by permission of the University of North Carolina Press.

New World, Known World

Introduction

—ⱲⱲ—

As for the fabled "antipodes," that is, men who occupy the other side
of the earth, where the sun rises when it sets on us; men who plant
their footsteps opposite ours: there is no reason to believe that such
men exist.

—AUGUSTINE, *The City of God against the Pagans*

For it may be truly affirmed to the honour of these times, and in a
virtuous emulation with antiquity, that this great building of the
world had never through-lights made in it, till the age of us and our
fathers. . . .

   And this proficience in navigation and discoveries may plant also an
expectation of the further proficience and augmentation of all sciences; because it may seem they are ordained by God to be coevals,
that is, to meet in one age . . . as if the openness and through passage
of the world and the increase of knowledge were appointed to be in
the same ages; as we see it is already performed in great part; the
learning of these latter times not much giving place to the former two
periods or returns of learning, the one of the Grecians, the other of
the Romans.

—FRANCIS BACON, *The Advancement of Learning*

These things I offer to your consideration (courteous reader) and require
you to show me the like in any part of the known world, if you can.

—THOMAS MORTON, *New English Canaan*

In an unidentified dedicatory poem to William Wood's *New England's
Prospect* (1634), the author praises Wood for having "Much knowledge
in so small room, comptly placed." My object in this book is to examine
the "rooms" of various shapes that several writers from the early period
of English colonization in North America built to accommodate what
Wood refers to as "personal and experimental knowledge" of the colonial

1

scene.[1] The period of my study runs from 1624, the year John Smith's *Generall Historie of Virginia, New-England, and the Summer Isles* was published, to 1649, when William Bradford presumably ceased working on his manuscript history of the Plymouth colony, now known as *Of Plymouth Plantation;* this period also saw the publication of Thomas Morton's *New English Canaan* and Roger Williams's *A Key into the Language of America.* These works are not all of a piece: Smith's book is an unstable blend of history and guidebook, Bradford's a relatively straightforward chronicle of events, Morton's a promotional tract with delusions of literary grandeur, and Williams's one of the more peculiar glossaries of a foreign language ever written. What they share in common is, first, that their authors had ties with New England in the first half of the seventeenth century (a matter of reconnaissance rather than residence in Smith's case, though he was after all the namer and first important promoter of New England); and, second, that they each want to render an organized account of a newly experienced colonial world that will make that world distinct from the one—"Old" or just generically familiar—that previously formed the ground of knowledge.

My inquiry into these texts and writers represents a sort of latter-day sequel to Wayne Franklin's *Discoverers, Explorers, Settlers: The Diligent Writers of Early America,* a book that predates the massive waves of literary-critical and ethnohistorical discussion on colonialism in the 1980s and 1990s—indeed precedes most of the work categorized as postcolonial theory—but remains one of the most thorough and probing attempts to treat early English colonial writing as being discursively subtle as well as deeply engaged with issues of language and knowledge. Early in his book, Franklin points out the idea that guides his work, and that carries over here: "More than anything else, the West [i.e., the New World] became an epistemological problem for Europe."[2] The English were relative latecomers in the history of Europe's transatlantic expansion, but they continued to struggle with that problem throughout their own development as a colonial power in North America and well into the period of the colonies' separation from the home country. Where Franklin's analysis of this struggle takes a decidedly metaphysical turn, becoming not so much a study of individual writers as a search for a kind of deep structure of primal American description, my own analysis will stick to more immediate considerations surrounding the task of shaping knowledge in the colonial period. I have opted for "shaping" over, say, "manufacturing," or "constructing" (words which in any case have received all the use in critical discourse that they need or deserve) not because "shaping" has any special theoretical weight but because it suggests the plastic, open-ended character of the knowledge projects represented by the texts in this book, projects that are crafted rather than engineered, and display the imperfections, quirks, and changes of purpose and direction that inevitably characterize the handiwork of single artisans.

A number of recent books concerned with the nature and history of discourse in various disciplines have employed the phrase "knowledge project" as a term of art, one that is usually not defined with any precision but tends to indicate an institutional or collective activity within a particular culture, the social sum of the various efforts to understand and define one kind of phenomenon or another.[3] I apply the same term to the texts in this book, but in a radically limited sense: the knowledge projects discussed in the following pages are the efforts of *individuals* to collect matter "of fact" for dissemination to those who might find it useful or educational, then to organize it into patterns and narratives that can be compared with and assessed against other patterns and narratives belonging to a particular society's fund of accepted knowledge. In short, a single writer molds a cluster of data, topics, and questions into a shape that can be appropriately "consumed" by other knowers. What is especially intriguing to me about this activity is that the shape chosen by the shaper so frequently depends on the use of literary conventions: the writer often appears to recognize that the authority and familiarity—the *dignitas*—of poetic or dramatic genres and of rhetorical tropes will serve to bring an appropriate order to the flood of new knowledge, will make it easier to digest. This reliance on the instrumentality of the literary will claim much of my attention in the chapters that follow.

The organizational work, literary and otherwise, that a writer undertakes in shaping knowledge proceeds under the assumption, historically endemic to European societies, that bodies of knowledge can be stably objectified,[4] as well as the more self-conscious assumption that knowledge has a concrete worth, that it is a medium of exchange that benefits both its maker and its consumer. A discussion of the first assumption is really beyond the conceptual scope of this book; the second assumption, though, can be illustrated from many sixteenth- and seventeenth-century texts, since the pursuit of (and commerce in) knowledge is one of the great preoccupations of the early modern period, up to and through the Enlightenment. I will offer a single representative example, from John Frampton's *Joyfull Newes Out of the Newe Founde Worlde,* his 1577 translation of the botanical guide to the Americas written by the Spanish physician Nicholas Monardes between 1569 and 1571.

Frampton dedicates his book to the courtier and poet Edward Dyer, who, along with Fulke Greville, inherited a share of Philip Sidney's library upon Sidney's death in 1586. Dyer was also associated with the Earl of Leicester and Christopher Hatton—both of whom, like Sidney, were interested parties in various colonial projects—and reputedly with John Dee, the famous mathematician, magician, and colonialist visionary who maintained a loose connection with Elizabeth's court throughout her reign. Interestingly enough, his most famous poem (made popular in William Byrd's musical setting from 1588) is "My mind to me a kingdom is," the first four lines of which are as follows: "My mind to me a kingdom is; / Such present joys therein I find / That it excels all other bliss / That earth affords or grows by kind."[5]

The dedication celebrates Dyer mainly as someone who is capable of appreciating the knowledge that Frampton is conveying by way of this book:

> And having finished the translation, I determined to dedicate my travail therein, to some rare lover of knowledge, for the worthiness of the work: and not finding any Gentleman of mine acquaintance, that was more studious, and more delighted with learned works, or that more cherished travelers, and lovers of all good knowledge: determined to dedicate the same to your worship before all others, requesting your worship to accept the work, and to be a patron of the same, and to take it into your protection, since the matter is of good substance, and of much value, and of me truly and faithfully translated into English.[6]

This is characteristic of sixteenth-century dedications in mainly being a plea for patronage; what distinguishes it to a degree is that Frampton is not asking for financial support simply on the basis of having commemorated Dyer's character and largesse by publishing a book dedicated to him. Rather, Frampton seems to be proposing something like a fair exchange: he, a fellow "lover" of knowledge, is bringing "matter of good substance, and of much value" to a customer who understands its worth, much like other "travellers" bring goods from faraway places to their eager clients. In return, Frampton would like to receive a fair price for his goods—perhaps to subsidize efforts to bring back more "Joyfull Newes" from the "Newe Founde Worlde." Frampton's dedication is one of many instances in the period of the treatment of knowledge as one of the staple commodities of the transatlantic world, with writers acting as the factors who make sure that such knowledge is transported appropriately to the "home market."

The movement of this peculiar commodity from producer to consumers was a socially complex process in the seventeenth century, as Andrew Barnaby and Lisa Schnell have suggested:

> To seventeenth-century thinkers, solutions to the problem of "right knowing" were intimately connected to a broader series of issues involving communities of knowledge and of knowers. Questions about how thought functioned, what constituted the conditions of right knowing, or how to attain a certain knowledge of things were inseparable from questions concerning the social contexts in which knowledge could be properly employed, the language that could be used to communicate truth in a public sphere, the claim to possess true knowledge (or even to participate in its discovery), and the right to be allowed subsequent access to it. At a larger level, all these questions were understood, in turn, as necessarily connected to the problem of order in human society, for epistemological claims were rarely viewed as free of broader sociopolitical significance.

Andrew Fitzmaurice has argued that such issues and questions were closely connected with a specifically humanist understanding of the power of rhetoric to form knowledge to certain ends: "Humanist culture . . . placed great emphasis upon the contingency of knowledge. In such an environment, in which knowledge was a matter of plausibility rather than certainty, the ability to persuade was crucial to social and political action."[7] Emerging from this environment, with its emphasis on the ethical, rhetorical, communal, and historical dimensions of "right knowing," the examples of colonial writing that I will be considering in this book bespeak immense challenges and difficulties. Every such knowledge project travels through a hurricane, so to speak, pressured from every side by belief, custom, and other forms of social code, by political, religious, and economic exigencies, by constraints on the conditions and modes of inquiry, by limitations on (and of) the writer, by the inertia of a language that resists the uses to which it is being put.

All of these pressures are exacerbated when the knowledge is, or is presented as, "new found."[8] In his seminal study of Columbus's conceptual universe, *The Invention of America: An Inquiry into the Historical Nature of the New World and the Meaning of Its History,* the Mexican philosopher Edmundo O'Gorman devised a parable (one perhaps inspired by Montaigne) that incisively outlined the problem:[9]

> We may compare the four continents with four human individuals, whose bodies are made according to the same biological model, something that they cannot change at will. But besides their biological existence each has a personal life, a unique and different biographical or spiritual being.
>
> Let us further imagine that, of these four men, three have always lived together, and that one of these three has the peculiarity of believing that the way in which he personally conceives the paramount ideals of human life has universal validity; his personal values are, to him, not subjective and relative, but objective and absolute. This man will naturally consider himself capable of determining the meaning or significance of the life of the other two men, of judging them by his own standards, thus setting himself up as the paradigm and the source of what constitutes true humanity.
>
> Now, suddenly, a fourth man appears of whom nothing is known. He is recognized as an individual of the human species, since his biological structure is obviously human. This is not sufficient, however, to identify the newly-arrived individual as a person, for though his physical appearance is that of a man, his spiritual being is unknown. So it was when America appeared on the historical horizon of Europe.

The gendering of O'Gorman's language here can, I think, safely be overlooked in favor of the power of his insight about the "peculiarity" of European culture at the earliest point of the early modern period. As J. H. Elliott observed in *The Old World and the New, 1492–1650,* his equally influential study of the reception history of the American discoveries, an "innate sense of superiority . . . has always been the worst enemy of understanding. How can we expect a Europe so conscious of its own infallibility—of its unique status and position in God's providential design—even to make the effort to come to terms with a world other than its own?"[10] The effort does eventually get made, but in ways that seem not to be informed by any obvious collective will; rather it is the sporadic, disconnected, and often troubled projects of individuals that begin to place the New World into a recognizable, and therefore assimilable, perspective for European observers.

These early encounters of Europeans with the Americas reveal—as vividly as any historic human situation, I believe—the intrinsic element of struggle in the effort to shape knowledge into forms that can be called either stable or permanent. Such projects more often than not display a jerry-built quality that tends to undermine whatever claims they make to provide definitive knowledge of people, things, places, and events. The effect bears a passing resemblance to Claude Lévi-Strauss's famous use of "bricolage" to describe the myth-making activities of primitive cultures:

> the rules of . . . [the bricoleur's] game are always to make due with "whatever is at hand," that is to say with a set of tools and materials which is always finite and is also heterogeneous because what it contains bears no relation to the current project, or indeed to any particular project, but is the contingent result of all the occasions there have been to renew or enrich the stock or to maintain it with the remains of previous constructions or destructions.

Colonial writing has an affinity with bricolage in that its "stock," the sum of materials and methods supplied by the writer's culture—"a collection of oddments left over from human endeavours," the "fossilized evidence of the history of an individual or a society"—is relatively static and rarely appropriate to the task at hand.[11] It differs, significantly, in not taking place in the closed system posited in Lévi-Strauss's analysis. The colonial writer does deal, indeed is forced to deal, with new things and not just with replicas and reflections of the old "stock." This has led several commentators to stress the ability of European colonists to improvise solutions based on the resources "at hand" to the problems posed by new knowledge, and thus to arrive at mastery of that knowledge.[12] Yet the impression of mastery is often conspicuously absent in the work of the colonial writers in this study. If as representatives of early modern Anglophone civilization they are not precisely equivalent to bricoleurs, their solutions to the problems raised by colonial experience, while functional by the standards of their society, can also be strange, awkward, inefficient, and even unadmirable according to those same standards.

The colonial archive—the archive of English-speaking colonists, at least—is a lengthy record of the gap that can arise between intention and result in the writer's work. It is a museum of bad form, faulty logic, uncertain rhetoric, tedious exposition, odd manipulations of style and genre. Franklin is again perceptive on the implications of the lack of "quality control" in these texts:

> American travel books tell us . . . about the enormous Old World energies which went into the attempt at controlling the West by means of the symbol system of language. As structures of language in their own right, they offer a double commentary on this general effort. And in their own imperfection as texts—their frequent lack of literary polish, their incompletion and outright loss, their often eloquent concern with the failures of verbal art—they portray that effort as at best a mixed success.[13]

These same qualities, though, are the source of my own fascination with colonial writing; for me the seams and flaws in such writing constitute a valuable index of what writing in general can and cannot do as a means of articulating the known world. For colonial writers inevitably engage in their knowledge projects with a sense of what writing *ought* to do, whether the individual writers can approach that goal or not. In the gap between the aspiration and the realization is the place where texts— and not just colonial texts—reveal much about how writers express what they know, or what they think they know, or what they want to know.

The fact that colonial texts are intellectually, politically, and aesthetically problematic requires no great skill to ferret out; it is a given—a point of departure. It opens up a range of questions that cannot be answered simply by focusing on the consequences of colonialism for the West. What did colonial writers think they were writing about? How did they think about the activity of writing itself? What models or precedents guided, and what constraints restricted, their participation in that activity? What topics loomed largest for them, and what topics did they tend to downplay or ignore? What kind(s) of audience(s) were they trying to reach? Finally, how do we readers of the present day (one kind of audience) think about these texts? What models, precedents, and constraints guide our reading of them? Is there a point at which the problem of readability in colonial writing shifts decisively from the text to the reader? I will not be able to answer these questions in every case, but I do want to raise them. One of my major interests in doing so is to shift the current emphasis, at least temporarily, away from colonial texts understood as elements in a discursive field back to such texts understood as the efforts of individual writers to articulate a historical phenomenon and their own involvement in it.[14]

I have two main reasons for trying to shift the emphasis in this way. First, the preoccupation in the last few decades with writing as a sort of circulatory fluid in the body of culture has led, I think, to an unnecessarily flattened account of the particular expressiveness of written work. Texts may be instrumental in delineating the space of cultural poetics, in creating notions of the self and other, in constituting or reinforcing ideologies. Yet the idea should not be lost that they are also the tangible efforts of persons to say, to mean, something about the world. There may be such a thing as collective (if not common) knowledge, but such knowledge has to rest on the projects of individual knowers. Texts cannot write the world, or write themselves into the world, without some very basic forms of human agency; someone always has to take the initial step of putting it down on paper, or whatever the available medium happens to be. No discussion of lost origins, oral transmission, anonymous authorship, transcription, collaboration, redaction, memorial reconstruction, editorial intervention, or compositors' quiddities can completely explain away either the moment of inscription or the fact that that moment is rarely, if ever, accidental.

My second reason is closely connected to my concern with restoring a sense of the individuality of colonial texts: I want to present an alternative to the commonly encountered mode of interpreting early European colonialism that assumes a kind of large-scale intentionality behind the process—as if, in the manner of the Roman Catholic Church throughout its history, the various parties to colonial activity had called a council to determine a doctrine of empire that would apply across national borders for the next few generations. I would argue that such an assumption is deeply, and even damagingly, anachronistic, that it represents an effort to read history backward in order to impose the systematic character of nineteenth-century imperialism as practiced by nation-states on the much more inchoate situation that existed several hundred years earlier. I think this sort of retrospective reading leads away rather than toward an accurate understanding of the processes of colonialism. Instead I would say that in order to arrive at a more accurate account of the historical and cultural phenomenon of colonialism—to be able even to arrive at a proper assessment of its tragic dimensions and terrible consequences—the critic must be sensitive to the fact that the participants in a particular event or set of events do not always know exactly what they are doing or trying to do. Accidents and mistakes are transformed into practices, and provisional solutions become policies, but the critic needs to remember that much of what people do in history is shaped by emergency, not foresight. In this sense, the work of early colonial writers is powerfully diagnostic of the general difficulty of forming a collective, coherent interpretation of a historical process at the time it is transpiring. Knowledge of the process emerges, when it emerges, only from the struggles of multiple individuals to know what it means.

Such struggles can hardly be called heroic. In fact, the texts that I am considering here, with the possible exception of Smith's *Generall Historie*,[15] can barely be said to have had any effect in the public sphere of the seventeenth century, either in Europe or in colonial North America. Morton's *New English Canaan* and Williams's *Key into the Language* are two of the rarest books in the colonial archive; neither was reprinted except as a historical artifact at a much later date (about 150 years later for *Key into the Language,* almost 200 for *New English Canaan*), and only a few original copies of either survive. What sort of audience these books reached in their own time is impossible to ascertain. Bradford's history of Plymouth remained in manuscript until the mid-nineteenth century, though various readers and scholars in New England had access to it from the 1660s until the Revolutionary War, when it was spirited away to England, eventually to resurface in the Bishop of London's library.[16] Even the relative popularity of the *Generall Historie* has to be weighed against Smith's enduring (and mostly undeserved) reputation as a mendacious historian.

These texts have still more basic failings; for one thing, they fail to create the well-defined order to which they aspire. They are afflicted with self-interest, naïveté, prejudice, and special pleading of various kinds. They occur moreover as elements of—as contributions to—an enduring crisis of knowledge in regard to Native Americans and, later, enslaved Africans. Yet, as I have already suggested, it is the flawed character of these efforts, the fact that they represent fairly unsuccessful knowledge projects, that makes them such compelling objects of study, for they are testaments to the great and abiding difficulty of transforming a new world into a known world. Moreover, each author's struggle to overcome that difficulty can and does generate writing of distinctive ingenuity and power—even, at times, of startling artistry. In the chapters that follow I will have frequent occasion to mark the creativity with language that emerges as part of the hard task of shaping the new world into a known one.

I turn now to the practical side of my inquiry. The traversal of these texts will involve a recurrent appeal to the notion of literary genre, though with some modification of the conventional sense of that term. Colonial writers are rarely devoted to a single genre; all of the texts under consideration here qualify as generically "mixed," and they are not atypical in this regard. They rely on a repertoire of verbal elements, not all of which rise to the level of self-contained genres but each of which can be considered a generic device that helps to bring knowledge into a particular order. What I see as the four most prominent of these devices (and of course one could go on to identify many others) will come under frequent scrutiny in this book, both in isolation and in combination.

Probably the most basic device is the inventory, encountered in a variety of forms in the colonial textual repertoire. Inventories can range from simple word lists to intricately categorized tables of peoples, plants, animals, minerals, exportable commodities, and so forth. At first glance, these inventories appear not to require much in the way of interpretation: they are simply to be read from top to bottom. On further examination, though, they often begin to suggest the presence of an implicit—one might say allegorical—organization, even something like plot. Hayden White's observation concerning the inventory-like character of medieval historical annals seems to be equally applicable to later uses of the inventory:

> there must be a story since there is surely a plot—if by "plot" we mean a structure of relationships by which the events contained in the account are endowed with a meaning by being identified as parts of an integrated whole. . . . The list of dates can be seen as the signifieds of which the events given in the right-hand column are the signifiers. The "meaning" of the events is their registration in this kind of list.[17]

Thus questions arise for the reader: Why are the items presented in this particular order? Why so many items in this category and so few in this other one? Why does the level of description vary? What has been included, and what is being left out? One of the most narrative-friendly forms of the inventory turns out to be that staple of colonial description, the English-Indian vocabulary, which reaches its apotheosis in Roger Williams's *Key into the Language.* But all of the texts here make use of inventories in some form, including *Of Plymouth Plantation,* the famous last item of which is a list of the passengers on the *Mayflower,* organized by household and accompanied by the vital statistics for each household during the thirty years after the first arrival.

In terms of creating a well-formed narrative of colonial activity, though, the most dominant device is surely history, understood both as *historia*—a story, a placing of events in contiguous sequence—and as *res gestae,* a recording of things that have happened, most commonly the deeds of human beings. Many colonial writers claim to be engaged primarily in writing this kind of history; yet the colonial setting also makes such history difficult to write. For Smith and Bradford, neither *historia* nor *res gestae* seems entirely adequate to the task of ordering the worlds of Jamestown and Plymouth, and my discussions of these two writers will turn on the problem of how conventional notions of history can come to be at odds with the demands of colonial description. I will argue at various points in this book that not only is the possibility of writing colonial history being put to the test, but the nature of history itself as well.

The third device, interestingly enough, is poetry, which crops up regularly in the work of Smith and Morton, and is crucial to the structure of Williams's *Key into the Language* (a text that remains, always, a special case). Passages of verse are inserted into colonial narrative to provide emphasis, reinforcement, or commentary, and to introduce or conclude various topics. Perhaps the main value of poetry in this context, however, is its power of authorization. Colonial writers are no different from other seventeenth-century writers in their tendency to look to the past for signs that their present projects are legitimate and worth pursuing, and poetry (whether ancient or modern) often functions as a marker of the authority of the past—the past, that is, of the Old World and its attendant social, cultural, and institutional networks; in short, the past as a form of privileged knowledge that bears directly on one's knowledge of the present. When a poem interrupts the flow of colonial narrative, the event is usually an invitation to readers to find analogies (if not typologies) that connect the new and the known. For this very reason, the introduction of poetry into the colonial text can be quite problematic, since analogy tends almost inevitably toward substitution. The poem becomes a symptom of the tendency of colonial writers to make sense of novelty by transforming it into something that, so to speak, has already happened.

Finally, and most importantly, there is dialogue, which I am thinking of here simply as the representation of a spoken exchange between two persons. This device figures both explicitly and implicitly in colonial writing. Smith, for instance, inserts a number of highly self-conscious dialogical set pieces into his account of his own activities in Virginia. But dialogue also has a way of creeping into relatively undramatic forums, such as word lists; Williams actually says that he has "framed" *Key into the Language* to suggest an "Implicit Dialogue."[18] There are even hints of a kind of dialogue in *Of Plymouth Plantation,* given Bradford's practice of juxtaposing quotations from letters and other documents representing different persons and differing points of view. Like poetry, dialogue carries the authority of past knowledge with it, since, going back at least to Plato and carrying on well into the seventeenth century, it is a favored vehicle for presenting discursive arguments on all manner of topics. At the same time, it has connections with theatrical performance and is thus tinged at least slightly with the element of heterodoxy so often detected—especially by Puritans—in Jacobean and Caroline drama. (The writer in this study with the greatest affinity for such drama, Thomas Morton, introduces verse passages and comic "characters" into the third book of *New English Canaan* in ways that evoke a court masque; at the same time, curiously, *New English Canaan* is more obviously dedicated to promoting a single point of view than the *Generall Historie, Of Plymouth Plantation,* or *Key into the Language.*) Dialogue may be the most poignant in effect of the four devices I have presented here, since a common iteration of it is one between a colonist and a Native American. Dialogue is also supposed to indicate the perspectives of two different persons; thus it also raises the possibility of two different, perhaps incommensurate, ways of knowing. In this sense it is perhaps more likely than the other devices to slip away from the writer's control and to compromise his efforts to bring order to knowledge of the colonial scene.

It is probably obvious by now that, in tracing the movements and interactions of these devices through various texts, I am also engaged in an effort to shape knowledge. What I would like to promulgate is knowledge of Anglo-American colonialism in which the familiar tools of literary interpretation play an essential role. The colonial past has been one of the main provinces of recent work in cultural studies, and colonial texts form one important set of "artifacts" within that work, but this does not necessarily mean that these texts are being read—by which I mean, read as if they were worth reading, as if they were more than a repository of illustrations and anecdotes for a broader argument about early modern society and culture. Often this argument is devoted to retrieving the testimony of the marginalized figures in the early colonial scene—the testimony of women in the Bay Colony, of Native Americans on the frontier, of slaves along the Piedmont. The limitations of my study will be obvious in this respect, and I frankly acknowledge them. At the same time, some types of knowledge projects are, textually speaking, not there to be reclaimed: female settlers did not produce descriptive or historical accounts of the first English settlements, nor did Native Americans or slaves write testimonies about early New England and Virginia for European consumption.[19] The attempt by literary critics (as opposed to archaeologists, social historians, and anthropologists, who benefit from a wider range of suitable evidence) to recover the silenced voices of the colonial period has tended to occlude what may, in the long run, be the more damaging problem: that

almost all of the texts of the early colonial period are, in effect, marginalized—little studied, little discussed, little understood. Yet without an understanding of these texts, one is easily reduced to relying on abstractions
and half-truths to describe the colonial past: "The Pilgrims were narrow-
minded prigs," for example, or "The Jamestown settlers were incompetent scoundrels." I continue to agree with Elliott's remark from some years
ago that

> in reality there are many [colonial] voices, among the conquerors and
> the conquered alike. We may not like what some of those voices are
> saying, but, as historians, we have an obligation to give a hearing to
> each and every one. There is no more crying need at this moment than
> to observe the observers with that same sensibility to historical context
> and environment which we pride ourselves on possessing when we
> come to reconstruct the world of the observed.[20]

In my view the "obligation" that Elliott describes has not diminished,
and it extends beyond the discipline of history proper to any other field
that purports to reach judgments on the colonial past.

Literary criticism, of course, is one such field, and one particularly well
suited to recovering the *energeia* of textual artifacts that, for one reason or
another, have become more difficult to "observe," as Elliott puts it. My
approach here, then, will be to take some extended time with works that
often seem opaque and intractable to present-day readers, in the belief
that study of these works as literary objects—as objects shaped by and
around metaphor, symbol, allegory, irony, affinity to genre, rhetorical
technique, poetic diction, the complex use of narrative and authorial
voice, and other such instruments in the writer's repertoire—enables a
kind of knowledge that adds to, but cannot be replaced by, the knowledge
gained from using the tools of history, anthropology, political science,
economics, or any other discipline. While we as inheritors of the English
colonial legacy can never hope fully to understand the convolutions, paradoxes, and catastrophes that accompanied the arrival of European settlers
on the North American continent, we can at least understand those
things better by paying close attention to both what and *how* some of the
earliest writers about the American scene wanted to know, and in turn
wanted their readers to know. This book is primarily an effort to attend to

the contours of such knowledge as it has been shaped by that endlessly powerful, flexible, and difficult tool, the written word.

I should briefly address several matters of organization and presentation. The sequence of material does not follow a strict bibliographical chronology, since in that case the chapter on Bradford would have to come last, due to *Of Plymouth Plantation*'s extraordinarily delayed date of publication. The discussion of that work also provides useful preliminary context for the chapter on *New English Canaan,* so I have moved Bradford ahead of Morton in this volume. In quoting from my selection of texts, I have modernized the spelling but not the punctuation or capitalization. The spelling of original titles I have generally left unchanged.

1

—∿∿—

The Incoherent Colonist

Troubled Knowledge in John Smith's
Generall Historie of Virginia

In the last book he published during his industrious career as a writer, *Advertisements for the Unexperienced Planters of New England, or Any Where* (1631), John Smith regularly advises his readers to refer back to the work he regarded as his magnum opus, *The Generall Historie of Virginia, New-England, and the Summer Isles* (1624), for a fuller account of matters that he could only touch upon in the fairly short text of the *Advertisements*. In the last chapter, for example, he says that

> because I cannot express half that which is necessary for your full satisfaction and instruction belonging to this business in this small pamphlet . . . I refer you to the general history . . . wherein you may plainly see all the discoveries, plantations, accidents, the misprisions and causes of defailments of all those noble and worthy Captains . . . with mine own observations by sea, rivers and land, and all the governors that yearly succeeded me in Virginia. . . . [W]ith it also you may find the plantations of Saint Christophers, Mevis [i.e., Nevis], the Barbados, and the great river of the Amazons, whose greatest defects, and the best means to amend them are yearly recorded, to be warnings and examples to them that are not too wise to learn to understand.

Throughout the *Advertisements*, Smith also ponders the fact that the *Generall Historie* and his other writings have not had the effect—for him and for others—that he wished them to have, and he makes remarks that fall somewhere between wistfulness and irony about his desire to have his work taken seriously:

> because I have more plainly discovered, and described, and discoursed of those Countries than any as yet I know, I am the bolder to continue the story, and do all men right so near as I can in those new beginnings, which hereafter perhaps may be in better request than a forest of nine days pamphlets.

Smith is altogether willing to attribute the neglect of his past work to the pigheadedness of the majority of people involved in the colonial enterprise, not least the separatists in New England, who "would not be known to have any knowledge of any but themselves."[1] But Smith's worry about the fate of his books carries over as a problem for contemporary readers, who—even if they take Smith seriously—still have difficulty giving their full attention to a work like the *Generall Historie.*

Why is this so? I think that the answer is quite straightforward in Smith's case: his books are simply not very well made, as either intellectual documents or literary artifacts. Yet this problem is also what makes them fascinating as objects of interpretation. Hastily prepared, often carelessly printed, they demonstrate a close—even close to transparent—relationship between Smith's struggle to arrange sentences and paragraphs and his struggle to organize facts and ideas into the kind of work that I have described in my introductory chapter as a knowledge project. In this sense the *Generall Historie* represents problems that can be found in many examples of seventeenth-century colonial writing, though not always in such an egregious form. For scholars and critics accustomed to mining underground to identify the conflicts and contradictions of thought in the early modern period, writing like Smith's opens veins of rich material close to the surface—which may help to explain the prominence of early colonial literature in the work of the new historicists, as well as its continuing use in cultural studies.

However, the relative ease with which the "code" of colonial texts like Smith's can be cracked to release cultural meaning has also led to a certain amount of skepticism about the whole enterprise. In a memorable exchange that occurred in 1993 across two issues of *Critical Inquiry,* Myra Jehlen and Peter Hulme debated the question of what constitutes appropriate interpretation of colonial texts, using the work of John Smith as their representative case. In her initial foray, Jehlen contends that critics like Hulme, by translating both the events and the documents of the colonial past into a discourse capable of literary-critical interpretation, turn out to be as deterministic as the procolonial scholars of previous generations. The crux for her is the issue of the historical reliability of colonial texts, or rather the lack thereof:

> Unreliability, if one thinks one understands its principle, can be decoded to reveal a narrative that now appears entirely reliable. The principle of unreliability in colonial narratives seems clear to many anticolonial historians today who, indeed, consider their work to be participating in a project of decolonization. Some of the resulting histories demonstrate the possibility for a radical uncertainty unanchored by material evidence to transmute [itself] . . . into an equal and opposite radical certainty.[2]

As a test to this "radical certainty," Jehlen offers a relatively well-known passage from the *Generall Historie,* in which Smith describes Christopher Newport's grotesque attempt in the autumn of 1608 to "crown" Powhatan as a sort of tributary monarch to James I.[3] Jehlen points out that "Smith describes a scene in which not just Newport but the English as a whole and their coronation ritual appear ridiculous. . . . The puzzle is why Smith punctiliously records a series of moves that make so solemn a white ceremony seem ludicrous?" The solution she proposes is that Smith is no more in full control of the facts of the event than Newport was of the actual ceremony:

> The self-deconstructing tendency of the coronation passage reflects its historical indeterminacies. Smith is uncertain about his situation, meaning that he is neither sure what the story unfolding around him is, nor how to tell it, nor even how he wants it to come out. So he effectively tells several stories composed of overlapping but not identical events.

Jehlen notes the curious resistance of the facts to Smith's attempts to interpret them: "These materials remain, as it were, undigested or semi-digested; they retain a quasi-independent and possibly rebellious life." In this state of affairs, she identifies a phenomenon that she calls "history

before the fact." Such history is anything but certain: the "lapses and in-
coherencies" of Smith's chronicles, "their redundancies and paradoxes,
represent the limits of discourse, the moments when discourse does not
know what to say." The problems that afflict a text of this sort, she concludes, also afflict its interpretation: "We [the critics] too write chronicles
of uncertainty, of which we are just the coauthors."[4] Therefore, critics
must be wary of being too sanguine about the reliability of their analyses
of colonial discourse.

In his response, Hulme defends his treatment of discourse as a form of
material fact that is not only useful but absolutely requisite to a responsible historical understanding: "The attempt to liberate history from discourse, and allow it some innocent space of its own is always doomed to
failure. However difficult the task may be, we always end up having to interpret the text." Hulme comments only in passing on Jehlen's approach
to Smith, but he does acknowledge "the importance of the *kind of writing*
. . . [she] *identifies* in Smith, which needs proper attention, and which may
well be a source of special significance." Jehlen's brief reply to Hulme returns to a disagreement that is stated circumstantially in her first essay
and more explicitly here: "Perhaps my major objection to focusing on
discourse is that it is a focus on coherence"—a coherence that, Jehlen
implies, is lacking in much of the colonial record.[5] Hulme and his contemporaries, she would argue, have transformed this record into a fluent
and logical "discourse" without genuinely taking account of its deeply
troubled, and troublesome, character *as* a record.

I will use this objection as a good place to begin thinking more inten-
sively about Smith's *Generall Historie,* and as a way of splitting the difference, so to speak, between Jehlen and Hulme. Both critics share a concern
with the problem of the incoherence of colonial history. In *Colonial
Encounters,* the book that initially prompted Jehlen's argument with
Hulme's historiographical method, Hulme treats the question as distinc-
tively "Virginian":

> There is little in Virginia's early history to give a satisfying sense of an
> "innermost propulsion" [here Hulme is using a phrase from Perry
> Miller] at work. Even worse, perhaps, Virginia had difficulty maintain-
> ing the coherence and integrity that its name hopefully suggested, the

proper boundary between "self" and "other" necessary to any establishment of national identity.[6]

The question that Hulme and Jehlen face equally, if from rather different vantage points, is how to make sense of such incoherence in its documentary forms; he would surely agree with her (as I also do) that "we always end up having to interpret the text." But how is one to go about this? Here Jehlen has some difficulty in articulating an alternative to the production of "radical certainty," other than to suggest the need to be more tentative about drawing conclusions from one's sources. In his response to Jehlen, however, Hulme is no more precise about the process by which one derives a coherent reading from an incoherent text.

I suggest that a constructive approach to this problem is to consider incoherence as a historical phenomenon in its own right, and as one that is as susceptible to analysis as any other such phenomenon—for if incoherence is a frequent feature of the written record of early modern colonization, then it needs to figure in a well-informed understanding of colonial history, whether that history is one of "discourse" or of "fact." Smith's *Generall Historie* is an apt vehicle for beginning such an analysis, since it stands as one of the least coherent of major colonial texts. Laboriously assembled by Smith from a haphazard collection of sources and published long after his return to England from Virginia, the book is full of internal contradictions, second- and thirdhand information, jarring juxtapositions of tone, and passages of uncertain authorship. Moreover, it attempts to narrate the history of Jamestown, one of the most chaotic, not to say distressing, "settlements" in the history of colonization.[7] It is a profoundly unsettled work, and in turn it unsettles efforts to characterize the activities in which Smith was so closely involved. Wayne Franklin has anticipated Jehlen's argument in pointing out that the *Generall Historie* is unable to settle into, or upon, a single narrative "voice":

> Captain Smith cannot tell the story he might like to, a tale of Virginian growth and promise, because too many other voices intrude on his. Those other voices not only have their own tales to tell, thus interrupting the flow of Smith's prose—they also undercut, with some subtlety, Smith's apparent assumption that the unity of English endeavor (should it ever be achieved) ought to be embodied in a unified account. If his

book as he presents it seems to sprawl, that very quality of its shape is significant of its meaning.

Franklin's discussion of the *Generall Historie* finds in it a vein of alienation that he sees running through most of the colonial literature of North America, arising from each writer's inability either to locate or to create a genuine sense of community in the colonial environment. Franklin associates this quality of alienation, once again, with the writer's "voice," describing that voice in terms that look forward to the lexicon of the new historicism: "each voice in these works is a center struggling for power, excluded in its own right but willing to exclude others, if need be, to fortify its own transcendent claims."[8] Franklin's most important insight about the *Generall Historie,* though, is that its sprawl has meaning; in other words, Smith's book is the formal (or we might say mal-formal) rendering of what Jehlen would call "radical uncertainty." To understand the precise historical character of Smith's uncertainty, which is to say his tendency toward incoherence, means understanding how it is manifested semantically.

I will argue, moreover, that the incoherence of a text like the *Generall Historie* immediately puts any construction of a discursive category like "seventeenth-century English colonialism" to the test. The interpretive practice I wish to bring to bear in Smith's case starts from the idea that texts are contrary beasts, that they resist assimilation into "discourse" as often as not, and that this contrariness needs to be acknowledged in any attempt to define what a discourse is and how it works. Such a practice seems to me especially necessary in trying to make sense of an area as historically fraught and as liable to reductive and ideologically weighted readings as the "discourse of colonialism."

A Globe-Like Jewel:
Smith's Ambivalent Knowledge

To get a better grasp of this quality of contrariness in Smith's work, I will forego discussing Smith's relationship with Pocahontas, a topic that has become something of a well-trampled hunting ground,[9] and focus initially on a passage taken from Smith's expansion of his earlier tract *A*

Map of Virginia (1612) in books 2 and 3 of the *Generall Historie;* these are the two sections of the larger work that most consistently show Smith's own hand as an author rather than as an editor. At the end of book 2, we find an Algonquian word list—in fact a duplicate of the one in *A Map of Virginia*. Modeled after a similar glossary in Thomas Harriot's *A briefe and true report of the new found land of Virginia* (1588), Smith's list mainly consists of common objects grouped loosely by kind: household items, weapons (the largest group), tools and raw materials, and features of land and water; the second half includes the Algonquian number system, as well as some chronological and theological terms.[10]

The list also contains two strange sequences of words and phrases, each contiguous, that suggest a hidden narrative underlying the otherwise colorless organization.

> *Weghshaughes,* Flesh.
> *Sawwehone,* Blood.
> *Netoppew,* Friends.
> *Marrapough,* Enemies.
> *Maskapow,* The worst of enemies.
> *Mawchick chammay,* The best of friends.
> *Casacunnanack, peya quagh acquintan uttasantasough,* In how many days will there come hither any more English Ships.
> . . . .
> *Tawnor nehiegh Powhatan,* Where dwells Powhatan.
> *Mache, nehiegh yourowgh, Orapaks.* Now he dwells a great way hence at Orapaks.
> *Uttapitchewayne anpechitchs nehawper Werowacomoco,* You lie, he stayed ever at Werowacomoco.
> *Kator nehiegh mattagh neer uttapitchewayne,* Truly he is there I do not lie.
> *Spaugtynere keragh werowance mawmarinough kekaten waugh peyaquaugh.* Run you then to the King Mawmarynough and bid him come hither.
> *Utteke, e peya weyack wighwhip,* Get you gone, and come again quickly.
> *Kekaten Pokahontas patiaquagh niugh tanks manotyens neer mowchick rawrenock audowgh,* Bid Pokahontas bring hither two little Baskets, and I will give her white Beads to make her a Chain.[11]

"Flesh" and "Blood" in the first excerpt occupy no clear category—they are preceded by the words for "Water," "Fish," and "Sturgeon"—but they convey a notion of the human body, both in its capacity for intimacy (as in the familial "flesh and blood") and as an object of violence (for here the two elements have been separated from the rest of the body). Immediately following these words are two nouns and two superlatives that would have been in common use among both colonists and Native Americans, and that could be applied as easily by either party to the other.

It is important to note, though, that Smith is translating Algonquian terms; in the immediate context, the primary object of the epithets "the worst of enemies" and "the best of friends" would most likely be the colonists. The question that ends the sequence—asked in hope, or anxiety?—appears to support such a conclusion. Even as Smith attempts to demonstrate a certain mastery of a non-European language, he also manages to suggest, perhaps unwittingly, that Powhatan's people might actually have opinions about the interlopers on their territories, and that those opinions might lead to significant decisions. The passage allows, in other words, for the existence of both consciousness and will among Native Americans.[12]

This same point emerges more dramatically, as it were, in the second passage. Again, Smith wants his readers to know that he can carry on a capable conversation in Algonquian, and perhaps he intends this example to show them the way an extended conversation would look and sound. Yet the utility of this passage for lay students of Algonquian is hard to detect, since it presents a singular exchange between Smith and the speaker(s); as a fragment of a historical moment involving Smith himself, it is unlikely to be duplicated, or even approximated, by anyone else. The interest of the sequence lies in its very impression of historicity, in the way in which it appears to represent a distinct exchange between Smith and the speakers of Algonquian. The nature of that exchange is extremely ambiguous: the informant is accused of lying, yet he may well be telling the truth; if he is lying, he may have a valid reason for doing so; the motives for the initial effort to locate Powhatan are never made clear. One is left with a sense of the caginess of both speakers, each deflecting the stratagems of the other.

One is also left with what is, upon the word list's initial appearance in *A Map of Virginia*, the first reference to Pocahontas in Smith's writings; the passage alludes to a banal if rather courtly material exchange, but also to an exchange that is commanded rather than invited: "*Bid* Pocahontas bring hither two little baskets." This is where the word list ends; the request for Pocahontas's presence receives no "answer." The whole excerpt suggests in a roundabout way the difficulty that arises when one attempts to render judgment on Smith's ideological position in relation to the Algonquians. The "Smithian" voice, though it may be peremptory, speaks here with no more authority than the Algonquian voice; indeed the voices seem to cancel each other out. Smith's mastery of a language does not extend in this instance to mastery of another culture.

This distinctive quality of Smith's voice emerges more directly in a number of his descriptions of personal encounters with the Native Americans. In book 3, chapter 6 of the *Generall Historie,* Smith recounts an ambush of one of his upcountry expeditions by the Mannahoacks, during which Smith's party captures a warrior:

> We demanded why they came in that manner to betray us, that came to them in peace, and to seek their loves; he [the warrior] answered, they heard we were a people come from under the world, to take their world from them. We asked him how many worlds he did know, he replied, he knew no more but that which was under the sky that covered him, which were the Powhatans, with the Monacans, and the Massawomecks, that were higher up in the mountains. Then we asked him what was beyond the mountains, he answered the Sun: but of any thing else he knew nothing; because the woods were not burnt.[13]

This remarkable display of comparative cosmography is probably intended to show the limitations of the Mannahoack worldview, yet Smith has neglected, for whatever reason, to suppress the irony at the heart of the exchange between indigene and interloper: the warrior understands rather too well who Smith's "people" are, and the resonances of their origin "under the world" would be inescapable to many, if not most, of the *Generall Historie*'s readers. What is perhaps most striking about the passage, regardless of the authenticity or fictiveness of the warrior's speech, is Smith's willingness to "quote" him, to allow him to speak in such an unvarnished way about the possible motives of the Europeans. It is surprising to find a voice from either side of the question advancing a claim that the colonial party is seizing a "world" from its rightful owners—and even more surprising to find that voice, and that claim, emerging from an allegedly "savage" source.

Possibly Smith is attempting to deflect the point of the Mannahoack warrior's observation by querying him on the boundaries of the world he knows; yet elsewhere the narrative displays a concern with the relative character of "the world," and the tension between Native American and European notions of its contents and its edges. Earlier in the *Generall Historie,* during the extended confrontation that leads up to Smith's rescue by Pocahontas (book 3, chapter 2), Smith tries to influence the chieftain Opechancanough through what could be characterized as the strategic deployment of European geographical lore:

> He [Smith] demanding for their Captain, they showed him Opechancanough, King of Pamunkey, to whom he gave a round Ivory double compass Dial. Much they marveled at the playing of the Fly and Needle, which they could see so plainly, and yet not touch it, because of the glass that covered them. But when he demonstrated by that Globelike Jewel, the roundness of the earth, and skies, the sphere of the Sun, Moon, and Stars, and how the Sun did chase the night round about the world continually; the greatness of the Land and Sea, the diversity of Nations, variety of complexions, and how we were to them Antipodes, and many other such like matters, they all stood amazed with admiration.[14]

Smith presents the compass to Opechancanough as a precious talisman, a "Globe-like Jewel," and indeed an ivory compass is considerably more valuable than the usual "trash" (to use Smith's own word for it) of glass beads, bells, and other trinkets that the Jamestown colonists used as barter in their traffic with Native Americans. Several pages later in the *Generall Historie* there is a particularly vivid example of this sort of barter and its practical consequences:

> Powhatan . . . fixed his humor upon a few blue beads. A long time he importunately desired them, but Smith seemed so much the more to affect them, as being composed of a most rare substance of the color of the skies, and not to be worn but by the greatest kings in the world. This made him half mad to be the owner of such strange Jewels: so that ere we departed, for a pound or two of blue beads, he brought over my king for 2. or 300. Bushels of corn; yet parted good friends.[15]

The narrative of the encounter with Opechancanough suggests that Smith recognizes the seriousness of his situation in presenting a gift that trumps blue beads by several orders of magnitude, an object of consider-able value to Smith himself. The compass certainly represents an ac-knowledgment of Opechancanough's high status within the Powhatan confederation. At the same time Smith uses the compass to lay his world against Opechancanough's, invoking that world in a kind of magical rit-ual that serves as both an assertion of Smith's own powers and a means of averting a possible catastrophe.

Moreover, Smith—indeed the passage as a whole—seems to revel in the magic inherent in a knowledge of the "roundness of the earth" and its "greatness," "diversity," and "variety" (a knowledge that seems to depend more on Ptolemy than on Copernicus, as is suggested by Smith's refer-ence to the "sphere of the Sun, Moon, and Stars," and his claim that "the Sun did chase the night round about the world continually"). The com-pass functions not only as a talisman but as a sign of the mysterious dis-tance between Smith's world and Opechancanough's: the chieftain's retinue "could see . . . plainly" the inner apparatus of the compass, "and yet not touch it." As "amazed with admiration" as Opechancanough's fol-lowers are, they fail to be entirely persuaded by Smith's magical geogra-phy: "Notwithstanding, within an hour after they tied him to a tree, and as many as could stand about him prepared to shoot him, but the King holding up the Compass in his hand they all laid down their Bows and Arrows."[16] Opechancanough finally relents, compass in hand, but the moment is a puzzling one: perhaps Smith's geography has rescued him from execution, or perhaps Opechancanough is simply expressing his gratitude for the lovely gift.

There follows a lengthy progress toward the residence of Powhatan, and ultimately toward Pocahontas's famous intercession. On the way, Smith witnesses a ritual in which the priests arrange meal, corn kernels, and sticks for a specific purpose; here again the narrative reflects a con-cern with the relativity of different versions of "the world":

> Three days they used this Ceremony; the meaning whereof they told
> him, was to know if he intended them well or no. The circle of meal
> signified their Country, the circles of corn the bounds of the Sea, and
> the sticks his Country. They imagined the world to be flat and round,
> like a trencher, and they in the midst. After this they brought him a bag
> of gunpowder, which they carefully preserved till the next spring, to

plant as they did their corn; because they would be acquainted with the
nature of that seed.[17]

Smith seems mainly concerned with pointing out the naïveté with
which Powhatan's people "imagine" their world; he reaches for the
homely, familiar image of the "trencher" to depict a flat world with the
people at the center. Yet the simile cuts another way, so to speak: if
Powhatan's people are in the middle of a serving platter, then they are
there to be eaten. Smith's analogy suggests nearly as much about the
colonist's model of the world as it does about the Native Americans'.
Even the "map" that the priests create, with its array of circles, bears comparison with Smith's account of "the sphere of the Sun, Moon, and Stars"
and its assumption of man existing "in the midst" of the universe. Like
Smith's world, the world of Powhatan's priests contains an element of
mystery: Smith must be "told" the "meaning" of the ceremony he is wit-
nessing—a ceremony that depends upon, and aims for, a privileged
knowledge not unlike the knowledge that Smith invokes when presenting
the compass to Opechancanough. The crucial difference between the two
worlds of English colonist and Native American comes down to the
means with which men occupy the center. The priests display a keen
knowledge of just where the difference lies, in their scheme to plant the
gunpowder "seed" in order to reproduce it for their own uses.

While the ceremony continues, Smith remains an object of intense
scrutiny among Powhatan's warriors: "more than two hundred of those
grim Courtiers stood wondering at him, as he had been a monster."[18]
The habitual order of things is now reversed—for the courtiers of
Elizabeth and James had enjoyed the spectacle of "monsters" from the
New World on several occasions; English expeditions from Martin Fro-
bisher's onward had typically returned with one or more captives, to be
paraded before the noble sponsors of such expeditions. As in the previous
encounter with Opechancanough, the Native Americans treat Smith not
as an omniscient magus but as an exotic, if threatening, curiosity, worth
the contemplation of a fairly large audience of the curious. The distinctions between English and Algonquian worldviews begin to dissolve into
a mélange of strangely similar motives.

What occurs at several points in the *Generall Historie*—or, more precisely, what Smith produces in his text—is an uncanny competition between worlds, a competition in which the victor is by no means obvious. One of the most striking examples of this occurs in book 3, chapter 10, in which Smith presents, in elaborately rhetorical fashion, his efforts to cajole additional food supplies from Powhatan. Though Powhatan seems to agree to provide the food to the colonists, he expresses considerable reluctance, telling Smith,

> some doubt I have of your coming hither; that makes me not so kindly seek to relieve you as I would: for many do inform me, your coming hither is not for trade, but to invade my people, and possess my Country, who dare not come to bring you corn, seeing you thus armed with your men.[19]

After more than a day of inconclusive negotiations with Smith's party, Powhatan delivers a more specific assessment of his situation, which Smith characterizes as a "subtle discourse" but which may strike us as pungently and painfully objective:

> What will it avail you to take that by force you may quickly have by love, or to destroy them that provide you food. What can you get by war, when we can hide our provisions and fly to the woods? whereby you must famish by wronging us your friends. And why are you thus jealous of our loves seeing us unarmed, and both do, and are willing still to feed you, with that you cannot get but by our labors? Think you I am so simple, not to know it is better to eat good meat, lie well, and sleep quietly with my women and children, laugh and be merry with you, have copper, hatchets, or what I want being your friend: then be forced to fly from all, to lie cold in the woods, feed upon Acorns, roots, and such trash, and be so hunted by you, that I can neither rest, eat, nor sleep; but my tired men must watch, and if a twig but break, every one crieth there cometh Captain Smith: then must I fly I know not whither: and thus with miserable fear, end my miserable life, leaving my pleasures to such youths as you, which through your rash unadvisedness, may quickly as miserably end, for want of that you never know how to find?[20]

It is remarkable enough that Smith portrays Powhatan in possession of such a clear-eyed perspective on the tensions that exist between his tribe and the Jamestown settlers; what is more remarkable still is that these speeches of Powhatan's are obviously literary constructions. Smith has chosen to include these speeches in his account—may in fact have created the speeches to fill out his narrative—with the simultaneous awareness that Powhatan's views are not strictly necessary to, or supportive of, the views that Smith is attempting to promulgate in the *Generall Historie*.

Bruce Smith uses these literary aspects of Powhatan's speech to reach a different conclusion, quoting from the speech at length but rationalizing it into relative insignificance within the *Generall Historie*. He argues that John Smith is following classical models for the insertion of orations into historical narrative, as in the works of Herodotus and Thucydides; that Powhatan's people are understood to be already conquered, thus their speeches have no real consequences; that John Smith is nodding toward the generic requirements of epic; that he wishes to demonstrate his own resourcefulness in, so to speak, out-rhetorizing Powhatan; finally, that he transforms the elements of Powhatan's primarily oral and sound-oriented world into writing and print, so that "the speeches no longer belong to Native American speakers; they belong instead to European readers. An aural event has been transformed into a visual event, and in that transformation it has changed ownership."[21] In sum, this is a latter-day variant of the subversion-and-containment thesis that figured so frequently in new historicist criticism. Yet nothing in the argument serves to account for the peculiar *energeia* of Powhatan's speech and others like it in the *Generall Historie*: their capacity for giving readers pause, for leading readers to recognize expressions of incongruity and uneasiness within the text. Surely Bruce Smith has responded to this very quality of Powhatan's speech in emphasizing it as he does.

John Smith is, of course, presenting Powhatan's words as part of a dialogue, and his own response within that dialogue is clearly intended as a refutation of everything that Powhatan has just said. His answer, however, is broadly rather than specifically dismissive, and concludes with more bluster than substance:

> As for the dangers of our enemies, in such wars consist our chiefest pleasure, for your riches we have no use: as for the hiding your provision, or by your flying to the woods, we shall not so unadvisedly starve

as you conclude, your friendly care in that behalf is needless; for we have a rule to find beyond your knowledge.[22]

As in the episode of the compass, Smith asserts his superiority on the basis of a hidden "knowledge"; at the same time this knowledge and its consequences remain crucially ungrounded. There is a practical reason for Smith's reticence: the "rule" is a pure fiction, improvised to deflect Powhatan's probing questions. Yet the *Generall Historie* regularly exposes Smith's knowledge as limited in various, and serious, ways; he is tied to the tree not only physically but epistemologically.

A poignant example of the boundaries of Smith's understanding appears in book 4, in the account of Smith's meeting in London with Uttamatomakkin, who had accompanied the newlyweds Pocahontas and John Rolfe on their visit to England in 1616; in effect, Uttamatomakkin was a spy, sent by Powhatan to determine the number and strength of the English nation, a task that quickly exhausted his patience. Here he turns to Smith to provide him with information that has so far eluded him:

> he told me Powhatan did bid him to find me out, to show him our God, the King, Queen, and Prince, I so much had told them of: Concerning God, I told him the best I could, the King I heard he had seen, and the rest he should see when he would; he denied ever to have seen the King, till by circumstances he was satisfied he had: Then he replied very sadly, You gave Powhatan a white Dog, which Powhatan fed as himself, but your King gave me nothing, and I am better than your white Dog.[23]

In Virginia, Smith was able to invoke "our God, the King, Queen, and Prince" as symbols of his power over Powhatan, but here he finds himself at something of a loss, for Uttamatomakkin has managed to reveal Smith's lack of access to the objects of Smith's own higher "knowledge."

Not only is Smith's God more distant than he seemed to be in Virginia, but Smith's vague answer to the rest of the query suggests all too clearly that he has had even less contact with the royal family than Uttamatomakkin has had. The remark "I am better than your white Dog" shows Uttamatomakkin bringing his own kind of knowledge to bear in measuring the distance between the cultures of King James and Powhatan, and his measurement is not necessarily flattering to James—or to Smith. Smith

must attach some significance to Uttamatomakkin's words, for he has included them in his account, but he neglects to comment on them in any
way, moving on instead to mention his many visits to Pocahontas with
"diverse Courtiers and others, my acquaintances," thus reminding his
readers—probably not to their complete satisfaction—that he is still a
man of affairs, though no longer the hero of Virginia.[24]

Mastery and Confusion: Smith's Voices

Smith is, after all, a writer of the early seventeenth century, and it has
been customary to think of his cultural and social milieu (at least on the
English side) as one where radically different ideas and values not only
collided with one another but somehow managed to survive the collision.
Yet there has also been a strong tendency among critics to treat seventeenth-
century colonial texts as representing the wreckage that remains after the
illusion of discordia concors collapses—the price paid, again, for such
texts not being very well made in the first place.

As critics have gone about rehabilitating works like Smith's (in the
sense that one would remodel a poorly finished house), what they have
claimed to discover, more often than not, is evidence of a hidden but entirely sturdy framework: a deeply authoritarian, thoroughly politicized
system of social control that continues to move toward a unitary aim—
the acquisition of greater power (or authority, or determination) for itself.
An example of the approach, and perhaps the definitive example of the
use of an early English colonial text in a literary argument, is Stephen
Greenblatt's highly influential essay from the early 1980s, "Invisible Bullets,"[25] which employs Harriot's A briefe and true report to portray a culture in the act of systematically repressing the alternatives that threaten
it, even at the moment when it appears to tolerate those alternatives.

In what is probably the most memorable part of this essay for most
readers, Greenblatt comments on Harriot's willingness to record the
Algonquians' ideas about the European contagions that circulated so de-
structively among them, and he presents several passages from A briefe
and true report that bear comparison with those I have quoted above from
the Generall Historie. The Algonquians regard the colonists as the spirits of
dead men in possession of living bodies; a number "who seem in histori-

cal hindsight eerily prescient," as Greenblatt says, predict that more Englishmen will come to kill and displace them; to account specifically for the devastating effects of introduced diseases, the Algonquians conceive an airborne spirit-army of vengeful colonists, slaying them with the eponymous invisible bullets.[26]

From this selection of passages Greenblatt raises the specter of a kind of radical relativism, an ideological chaos flowing beneath Harriot's attempts at objective description:

> For a moment, as Harriot records these competing theories, it may seem to us as if there were no absolute assurance of God's national interest, as if the drive to displace and absorb the other had given way to conversation among equals, as if all meanings were provisional, as if the signification of events stood apart from power.

As quickly as Greenblatt invokes this apparition, he dissolves it, for it does not square with his severe conception of colonial history. The broaching of alternative viewpoints, Algonquian or otherwise, is actually a feature of what we might call "counterintelligence," an indication that the internal security arm of a hegemonic culture is doing its job:

> power thrives on vigilance, and human beings are vigilant if they sense a threat; in part that power defines itself in relation to such threats or simply to that which is not identical with it. . . . English power in the first Virginia colony *depends* upon the registering and even the production of potentially unsettling perspectives.

Thus both Harriot's quasi-anthropological curiosity and his apparent openness to letting Native Americans "speak" in his narrative are redefined as forms of hostility toward those things that power has not yet come to possess as its own:

> The recording of alien voices, their preservation in Harriot's text, is part of the process whereby Indian culture is constituted as a culture and thus brought into the light for study, discipline, correction, transformation. The momentary sense of instability or plenitude—the existence of other voices—is produced by the monological power that ultimately denies the possibility of plenitude.[27]

Greenblatt's account here depends crucially on the assumption of a generalized bad faith, as if Harriot's use of Native American voices must necessarily be disingenuous—whether or not Harriot, both the agent and the captive of the dominant culture, is conscious of that disingenuousness. This is certainly an easy enough conclusion to reach, given the subsequent history of English relations with Native Americans. The same charge of disingenuousness could as easily be leveled at Smith when he records the "alien voices" of Powhatan's people at the edges of Jamestown almost forty years later. The problem here, of course, is that the textual evidence for the attitudes of either Harriot or Smith is highly ambiguous. Would it not also be possible to claim, based on the same quotations, that Harriot and Smith really *did* respect the qualities of the Native American cultures they encountered? Yet such a claim seems more than a little naive, especially in Smith's case.

The difficulty here brings me back again to the matter of coherence in the Jamestown colony. A colony is a project, and a project of any sort succeeds or fails based on the ability of its "projectors" to organize the materials, both concrete and conceptual, that they have gathered together in order to make whatever kind of thing they intend to make. A coherent project, in other words, emerges from the projectors' mastery of a body of data. Yet such a project would confront a paradox that also, quite obviously, affects every effort to think historically, and that involves the disjunction between what I will call comprehensive mastery and critical mastery. Is data mastered by knowing and using all of it (at least as much of it as can possibly be known and used), or by recognizing and selecting what is most important for the work at hand? Probably most efforts to build coherent projects include aspirations toward both kinds of mastery; at the same time, critical mastery is more likely to be favored as the most crucial aspect of such project building, if only because of its practical advantages.

This distinction may help to unravel some of the cognitive tangle surrounding Smith's description of his own activities. The *Generall Historie* appears weighted heavily toward comprehensive mastery; it is not that the signs of critical mastery disappear altogether, but that they are subsumed within Smith's effort to embrace the whole history of the Virginia enterprise in his writing. That history in turn suggests the desire of the

Jamestown settlers to master the New World comprehensively—to acquire, and allow for, all the possible "versions" of the Virginia colony, from an earthly paradise to a vast tobacco farm, from a gentleman's parade ground to a paradigm of military empire. While the Massachusetts Bay Colony maintained a built-in selection principle based on the theocratic beliefs of its founders, the colonial society in Virginia found itself unwilling to choose between its many potential meanings, thus setting many of its members against Smith, who, as an actor in the history (as opposed to a writer *of* the history), made much of his powers as a critical master of the situation at Jamestown.

The problem with comprehensive mastery, of course, is that it is fatally open-ended, offering as it does an infinitely receding horizon of data still to be acquired. When this desire to master everything is acted out on the historical field, it can degenerate rapidly into a near-total loss of control, under which the very notion of mastery loses any significant meaning. This loss of control is reflected in Smith's history as well—or perhaps it would be more accurate to say that Smith constantly struggles with his control of the historical data in his efforts to comprehend the comprehensiveness of the collective experience at Jamestown. The effects of this struggle are more positive in the *Generall Historie,* however, than the effects of the struggle over control at Jamestown itself.

If Smith the writer is viewed as working toward an ideal of comprehensiveness, toward a truly "general" history, then his account of his relations with Powhatan's people becomes less disorienting—if, perhaps, only somewhat less. Examples of the pursuit of this ideal are frequent in England during the late sixteenth and early seventeenth centuries: Philip Sidney's *Arcadia,* Edmund Spenser's *The Faerie Queene,* Richard Hooker's *Of the Laws of Ecclesiastical Polity,* Michael Drayton's *Polyolbion,* William Prynne's *Histriomastix,* Walter Ralegh's *History of the World,* and Robert Burton's *The Anatomy of Melancholy* are all notable instances, each in its own way. The issue is not that Smith is constitutionally unable to make critical distinctions or to identify internal contradictions among the many voices in his work, but that, given the nature and intellectual background of his project, he does not view such activities as relevant. The *Generall Historie,* in other words, is a vivid example of "undialectical" writing and thinking, and its character in this respect has less to do with the technical deficiencies of its author than with the cultural conditions under which he operated, both in Virginia and in the world of words to which he returned in England after suffering the near-fatal injuries that ended his career as a colonist.[28]

As difficult as it would be to claim Smith's attitude toward Native Americans is sensitive and respectful, it would be equally difficult to claim that it is bigoted and intolerant. His attitude seems, strangely enough, to take in both of these possibilities. What is perhaps most unsettling about this—to return to the adjective that I used at the outset—is that Smith displays no obvious intellectual discomfort over appearing to occupy two contrary positions at the same time. Powhatan as friend and as enemy, as oppressor and oppressed, as wise man and as foolish savage, as subject and as object, as figure of likeness and of otherness—Smith makes room for all of these possibilities in his narrative and does not rely consistently on any one of them. In the *Generall Historie,* equivocation is transformed into a literary and historiographical mode.

Again, this is not just a matter of Smithian idiosyncrasy. It is the same quality that Greenblatt perceives and finds so disturbing in Harriot's *A briefe and true report:* a willingness to straddle both sides of the line, to which the reader responds by invoking, as if by force of nature, the name of Niccolò Machiavelli. What readers such as Greenblatt have sought, however, is not a formal connection with *Il principe* but a dialectical model that will expose "instability" and "plenitude" as mere illusions. Thus the potential anarchy in Harriot's account is, in a curious way, moralized. Greenblatt's essay raises, but cannot allow for, the possibility that instability and plenitude might be the dominant qualities of Harriot's thought—that in Harriot's effort to "think" Virginia, to master it comprehensively, confusion reigns in a very significant way. To accept this notion would be to experience a sort of epistemological vertigo; Greenblatt instead contains it within a structure of determinate political relations where it becomes, as it were, only a dream of falling.

Yet I think this notion must be accepted, if only because so much of the record of sixteenth- and seventeenth-century English colonization belongs to Harriot's, and Smith's, way of thinking. This record presents a history of competing rationales, in which the models for English activity in the New World run against each other in disorderly fashion, like ships torn from their moorings. There is nothing unusual about Smith's inability to "navigate" in a single direction in the *Generall Historie;* it is a characteristic feature of colonialist description in the period. As Fitzmaurice has noted, early English colonial promotion "employed a whole battery of frequently conflicting arguments." Not only were these arguments "incoherent between authors and across time," but also "often the same author would resort to a range of mutually contradictory arguments."[29]

For example, in the manuscript known as the *Discourse of Western Planting,* written in 1584 to promote Ralegh's Virginia expedition, Richard Hakluyt the Younger presents widely different models of colonial activity in the space of a few pages. Although he makes much of missionary enterprise among Native Americans, his primary emphasis is on establishing trade relations:

> after the seeking the advancement of the kingdom of Christ, the second chief and principal end of the same [western discovery] is traffic, which consisteth in the vent of our clothes and other commodities of England, and in receiving back of the needful commodities that we now receive from all other places of the world.

Such trade will require fortified factories, to fend off French, Spanish, and Portuguese competitors; but these fortifications grade rapidly into a rather more militant variety: "we are to plant upon the mouths of the great navigable Rivers which are there, by strong order of fortification, and there to plant our Colonies. . . . And these fortifications shall keep the natural people of the Country in obedience and good order." Hakluyt then proposes a decidedly Machiavellian sort of diplomacy as a way of expanding the colony's size and power:

> if the next neighbors shall attempt any annoy to our people . . . we may upon violence and wrong offered by them . . . enter into league with the petite princes their neighbors that have always lightly wars one with another, and so entering league now with the one, and then with the other we shall purchase our own safety and make ourselves Lords of the whole.

Later, "admitting the worse that people will neither receive our commodities, nor yield us theirs again," Hakluyt suggests an alternative approach that will allow the colonists to "become great gainers will or nill the natural inhabitants of those Regions or others: And that is by enjoying certain natural commodities of the lands infinitely abounding in no account with them and with us of great price."[30] In these passages, Hakluyt presents a series of particular responses to contingent situations, but he provides very little sense of the relations between his responses: the rationale that would include both peaceful trading and mercenary warfare, both a strong defensive (if not offensive) posture and the enjoyment of commodities "in no account with" Native Americans, is never very clear.

A similar sort of confusion emerges in Ralegh's *Discoverie of the Large, Rich and Bewtiful Empyre of Guiana,* written twelve years later. Late in this account of his abortive voyage into the Orinoco River basin in 1595, Ralegh hints that the English, by establishing a military force in South America, may ultimately be able to restore the Incas to their rightful domain; in support of this, he cites an apocryphal prophecy: "from *Inglatierra* those *Ingas* should be again in time to come restored, and delivered from the servitude of the [Spaniards]." In return for the services of this English militia, the Inca emperor "would yield her Majesty by composition so many hundred thousand pounds yearly, as should both defend all enemies abroad, and defray all expenses at home, and . . . he would besides pay a garrison of 3000 or 4000 soldiers very royally to defend him against other nations." After proposing this elaborate scheme, in which installments of Inca wealth serve to balance Elizabeth's books, Ralegh reverts almost immediately to a much cruder approach: the Inca emperor "hath neither shot nor Iron weapon in all his Empire, and therefore may easily be conquered."[31] Here Ralegh briskly dismisses the distinctions to be made between arguments for "protection" and arguments for conquest—probably because for him, as for Hakluyt, the distinctions did not hold.

At this point, I hope that it is becoming clear that Smith's writing, for all its quirkiness, belongs within an intellectual tradition based not so much on fixed generic expectations as on persistent habits of mind, a tradition that the *Generall Historie* not infrequently represents with great rhetorical and narrative force. As Gary Nash has pointed out for the southern colonies and Richard Johnson for New England, English attitudes toward the Native Americans were decidedly heterogeneous, and they continued to evolve throughout the colonial period.[32] The gradual hardening of policy had more to do with responses to the pressure of historical accidents (such as the relative success of Opechancanough's assault on the colonists in 1622) than with any sort of well-defined, or even poorly defined, imperialistic program imported from England.

It would be more accurate to say that the colonists imported a multiplicity of approaches that only sorted themselves out over the *longue durée*. In the first volume of his massive study *The Shaping of America,* the geographer D. W. Meinig distinguishes among eight specific phases of colonial activity—exploration, gathering, barter, plunder, outpost, imperial imposition, implantation, and imperial colony—with the first five phases belonging to what Meinig calls the "prelude" and the last three to "fixation." Though Meinig says that "this is not a rigid sequence," he suggests that one phase leads logically into the next in most instances. The model is a useful one, but I think it is also important to recognize that the various stages could and did occur simultaneously or in different orders; and in the literature of colonization, the rationales for these phases could coexist without one rationale necessarily dominating the others. Meinig also points out that the sequence leads to different outcomes: the indigenous inhabitants might be expelled beyond a "firm frontier" (Virginia); they might establish a mutually beneficial trading economy with the Europeans (Canada); or they might fuse in various ways with the colonists to create a polyglot culture (Mexico).[33]

Quite possibly these outcomes were the result of the distinct cultural traditions and expectations of the three colonial powers in the Americas: an English colony by both nature and nurture would not be likely to mirror its French or Spanish counterpart. Yet each power was constantly—one might even say neurotically—aware of the colonial activities of the other two and used those activities as models (albeit often in a negative or distorted form) for its own. In any case, caution should be exercised in any effort to isolate a single, stable version of colonialism out of the flux that surrounds the early English activity in North America. I agree with Michael Warner's position: "colonial discourse has no more unity than colonialism. To speak of it in the singular hypostatizes a political intention that belongs to no one." Warner argues further that such discourse "is at best a retrospective mapping of sometimes overlapping but sometimes incommensurate contexts."[34] Perhaps a better project would be to try to describe more accurately such overlapping contexts as well as the conflicts they generate.

But mapping chaotic terrain is always a challenging enterprise. We may be the critical readers of the new millennium, but we still find it difficult to accept forms of cognitive activity (which, in historiographical terms, is as much as to say forms of textual activity) that appear to function neither dialectically nor monologically. We hesitate in the face of historical situations in which the actors, *compis mentis* and in all apparent innocence, can embrace starkly conflicting premises as if these premises were equally valid and efficacious. This raises (as it does for Greenblatt, who quickly dismisses it) the prospect of an extreme relativism at work under the external certainties of the English Renaissance, and it leads to what in the current parlance would be termed an "aporia."[35]

Yet the fall into relativism implies a predisposition toward doubt ("If x is untrue, than why not y and z?"), which Smith, for one, does not demonstrate to any significant degree. He accepts without hesitation the harsh conventions of colonialism, as in his conclusions regarding the 1622 massacre in book 4 of the *Generall Historie*:

> it is more easy to civilize them [the Native Americans] by conquest than fair means; for the one may be made at once, but their civilizing will require a long time and much industry. The manner how to suppress them is so often related and approved, I omit it here: And you have twenty examples of the Spaniards how they got the West-Indies, and forced the treacherous and rebellious Infidels to do all manner of drudgery work and slavery for them, themselves living like Soldiers upon the fruits of their labors.

Karen Ordahl Kupperman has pointed out that Smith's opinions became more reactionary over time, as he came to rely on his memories and on secondhand information rather than on any concrete experience of conditions in Virginia. A passage like the one above is "a caricature of his earlier views."[36] Yet while there is not much uncertainty on display here, there is still a certain dissonance in the passage; even in presenting the Spaniards as exemplars, Smith displays a certain amount of scorn at the way they have acquitted themselves, "living like Soldiers" upon the "drudg-ery work and slavery" of Native Americans. Throughout the *Generall Historie,* Smith has contended that the desire of the settlers to live "like Soldiers" in this fashion—through pillage, and extorted labor—is the source of many of the problems at Jamestown.

Another interesting qualification occurs shortly before the passage I have just quoted: Smith, drawing his account of the massacre largely ver-batim from Edward Waterhouse's *A Declaration of the State of the Colony and Affaires in Virginia* (1622), interrupts an expostulation on the general cowardice of the Algonquians with a parenthetical remark: "But I must tell those authors, though some might be thus cowardly, there were many of them had better spirits."[37] Smith, here as elsewhere, speaks not with one voice but with many voices; each voice speaks with authority and conviction; each voice speaks "the truth." The text is pulled toward con-tentious dialogue even when Smith is not explicitly creating speeches in the text for his contending historical actors.

What to make of this? Faced with the task of finding order in the midst of disorder—for this is, after all, the perennial task—most contemporary critics of early colonialist literature have opted for what Hayden White would call the ironic reading of the historical record.[38] This usually in-volves excavating what is hidden according to one of the many formula-tions of concealment that are now available; and what is almost always exposed to view is a monological vision of reality, which the text has art-fully masked or dispersed but which the careful use of dialectical method has brought to light. This may indeed prove satisfactory for many kinds of texts, and for many periods and types of cultural activity—but not, it seems to me, for Smith's *Generall Historie* or for much of the colonialist lit-erature written in North America and England in the late sixteenth and early seventeenth centuries.

It would be highly impractical for critics to dispense with dialectical method (certainly I will not have done so in this book), but I would argue for an effort to read colonial writers less ironically and to acknowledge a state of affairs corresponding to Jehlen's assertion that present-day critics are "coauthors" of "chronicles of uncertainty"—that thinking the thought of the past is an immensely challenging task.[39] Smith, very much a man of his time, would almost certainly demur at attempts to associate his mixed rationales with more recently developed conceptions of pluralism. His work is dialogical in ways that cannot be perfectly replicated or reconstructed, thus forcing present-day readers to take up one of the most ancient and difficult of historiographical and critical tasks: thinking one's way across a distance that belongs to the fourth dimension. This distance is the one aporia that really matters.[40]

Part of the challenge for literary historians is simply to take the distance seriously, to grant to Smith's text and to others like it the sort of powerful otherness that is attributed routinely to more conventionally literary texts—which is to say, the otherness of minds not one's own, observed in the difficult act of representing the world on paper. Whether it corresponds to Jehlen's "history before the fact" or indicates something else, Smith's account of Jamestown in the *Generall Historie* represents the progress of colonization on this continent, with all its attendant and enduring agonies, as less a matter of the evil in people's hearts than of the confusion in their minds and their words. For this reason if for no other, Smith's own confusion deserves—indeed, rewards—the close attention of his readers.

2

—∿—

Silent Partners

Historical Representation in William
Bradford's *Of Plymouth Plantation*

William Bradford's manuscript annals of the Pilgrim settlement in Massachusetts, a text now universally known as *Of Plymouth Plantation,* may have many advantages over John Smith's *Generall Historie* in terms of its basic narrative coherence, yet like Smith's book, it is a difficult work—difficult to read from end to end and difficult to comprehend as a whole. It remains simultaneously one of the most and one of the least readable texts from the early colonial period. Bradford receives praise for his unusually personal and varied style, his humor, his talent for balancing piety and pragmatism; for these reasons, as well as for the contributions of Bradford's book to a particular form of American mythology, *Of Plymouth Plantation* is more often studied and taught than the works of Bradford's near-contemporaries in the Massachusetts Bay Colony, and probably any other Anglo-American text from the same period. Even so, it hovers uneasily between history and memoir, public and private discourse, theological and secular narrative; its relation to genre is always in question, since it offers no very precise fit with most of the conventional categories. Like Smith before him, Bradford faces the problem of mastering a disparate set of records and testimonies that reflect various, frequently competing perspectives and refer to events and circumstances that have receded in both time and memory. To compound the problem, Bradford, like Smith, must deal with the paradoxical plight of the eyewitness, which is to have the most direct access to a particular history but rarely the most objective and dispassionate view of it. And as is the case with Smith, Bradford chooses comprehensiveness over selectivity in seeking to gain control of his materials, including much more of the available archive than is strictly necessary to make his historical "argument."

Unlike Smith, however, Bradford must also organize and write his historical narrative in the full view (if not always under the tight influence) of the doctrinal imperatives of his religious community. This latter aspect of Bradford's position has obviously attracted the lion's share of attention and shaped the direction of critical discussion over the years, so that the narrative and rhetorical unevenness of the text has tended to be understood as indicating less the general difficulty, confronted by many colonial writers, of shaping historical knowledge into coherent form than the specific difficulty for Bradford of hewing cumulatively to the lines of a demanding theological template during the many years he worked on his manuscript. The prevailing view appears to be that *Of Plymouth Plantation* is a providentialist history gone awry, that the much longer second book reflects Bradford's disappointment at the gradual dissolution of the Pilgrim community and the loss of its original mission. Robert Daly's remark is typical: "Bradford's history," he says, "begins magnificently, diminishes into a tedious account of unsorted administrative details, and ends, uncompleted, in silence."[1] The loose narrative structures and convoluted digressions of the annals are thus (so the argument goes) a form of mimesis, depicting not only the community's decline from an ideal that is presented with great passion and force in the first book, but also Bradford's cumulative disquiet and bewilderment as a witness to and participant in that decline.

Several of Bradford's readers, including David Levin, Alan Howard, and Walter Wenska, have argued eloquently in defense of Bradford's method in the second book, but the shadow of the earlier interpretation falls over these efforts as well, for they mainly defend Bradford against the charge that for much of that book he is not writing very good providentialist history. Howard, Levin, and to an extent Wayne Franklin represent the "Augustinian" school of Bradfordian criticism, in which Bradford is portrayed as deeply conscious, sometimes to the point of melancholy, of the incapacity of sinful humanity to fulfill God's purposes on Earth; the second book then becomes an inquiry into this very incapacity. Mark

Sargent draws on the same strand in suggesting that the body of Bradford's history constitutes a "quiet confession" of the tensions within the separatist movement, tensions that became more poignant due to the sea change in English attitudes toward separatism in the wake of the Civil Wars, and that Bradford tried to address more fruitfully in his late *Dialogues*. But all such readings assume that providential design looms in the background of the second book, functioning as a spiritual and moral benchmark even if humanity fails to move toward it.[2]

In this chapter, which will proceed from a comparative look at the first book to the consideration of several features (as well as persons) of the second and include a side-glance at an important factor in the historical background of the Pilgrims' activities, I will argue that the case I have outlined above has been greatly overstated—that in the second book, Bradford is not actually attempting to write providential history. The impatience that Bradford's readers frequently betray with the second book seems to arise from a misapprehension of one of its most obvious features, a feature that William Haller long ago noted in passing when he remarked that Bradford "writes, as he goes on, less and less like a Puritan preacher and more and more like the author of *Robinson Crusoe*," and that one of my students summed up quite aptly when he called *Of Plymouth Plantation* "a New England *Bleak House*."[3]

It is an account, that is, of a complicated, difficult, inconclusive business enterprise carried out over a period of many years, and on which Bradford reflected for many years. As a knowledge project it represents Bradford's attempt to organize and rationalize the multiple aspects of this activity within a traditional historical framework. Its intrinsic interest is in the details and intrigues of that business and its effects on the community in which it was transacted. John Griffith, one of a few critics to pay close attention to Bradford's preoccupation with commerce, believes that this preoccupation affects the style of the book in a more general way: "Bradford's work distills a great part of human affairs into a kind of semiexplicit bookkeeping, in which assets are weighed against liabilities with an eye primarily toward the total balance." Griffith wants to absorb Bradford's economic concerns into another type of providentialist reading, involving a quasi-Weberian triumph of godly capitalism. More conservatively if also more subtly, Kenneth Hovey perceives in the "mundane and practical character" of the second book a demonstration of the notion that, "[i]n a world devoid of miracles, God can still be seen in the success of weak means."[4] But to describe Bradford as yet another apologist for either a "hard" or a "soft" Protestant work ethic is to neglect the characteristic uneasiness of the second book's organization and tone. The second book does manage to provide moments of reflection on the ways of Providence; however, these moments cannot be extrapolated to form a satisfactory providentialist reading of the whole.

During the long period of the manuscript's composition, Bradford seems to have become quite aware that the providentialist perspective was not well suited to the material at hand. The most obvious evidence for this is his decision to present this material in annalistic form, convenient for marking the exigencies and discontinuities of worldly time but not for observing the serene progression of "cosmic" time toward the Apocalypse. Jesper Rosenmeier notes as part of his largely providentialist interpretation of Bradford that "The annals are filled with extraordinary scenes from the history of Plymouth's salvation; but they do not stand as parts of a great and coherent whole, as actions in an evolving drama. The years are shining but isolated moments, beads of revelation that remain unstrung."[5] Accounts of the vagaries of commercial activity rarely make for rewarding reading as evidence of God working out his plan in human history; hence the conclusion that the second book is both disappointed and disappointing. But this may only indicate the disappointment of readers at encountering the inapplicability of a favored thesis.

I will instead propose that the main problem confronting Bradford, and consequently Bradford's readers, in the second book of *Plymouth Plantation* is one that is endemic to the writing of *secular* history in a colonial setting, one that could be considered a problem of modern history in general. This is the problem of describing what might be called "corporate life," accounting for a collective entity and for the passage of that entity through time—as well as through an unfamiliar landscape in which the boundaries and interior relations of particular kinds of European communal life have to be defined anew in the face of unusual pressures from both without and within. Bradford as historian must adjudicate between an account that emphasizes the entity, the body politic of Plymouth Colony (a body with an implied interior life that can be represented metonymically through the lives of its individual members), and an account that emphasizes the outward activity of the entity, which extends beyond the entity itself and takes on a life of its own, though often in a much less "personal" and easily accessible sense.[6] It is the character of this other "life," and Bradford's response to it, that I will try to explore in the discussion that follows. First, though, I want to consider in more detail the conventional understanding of the first book as a benchmark of providentialist historiography.

Providentialism and Historical Form in the First Book

The problem of describing Plymouth's corporate life appears not to weigh very heavily on Bradford in the first book, which *is* more unified and uniform, and certainly more self-assured, in its presentation of a community gathering itself together

> into a church estate, in the fellowship of the gospel, to walk in all His ways made known, or to be made known unto them, according to their best endeavors, whatsoever it should cost them, the Lord assisting them. And that it cost them something this ensuing history will declare.

As this last sentence suggests, the evidence of narrative design is fairly obvious in the first book. Bradford orders his material not only chronologically but teleologically, into chapters that are organized topically as well as in terms of sequences of events, and he indicates in numerous ways that his history is plotted and moving toward a particular outcome. He alludes to his "intendment" and to his (sometimes unsuccessful) efforts to manage and prune his ample material: "it is not my purpose to treat of the several passages that befell this people whilst they thus lived in the Low Countries (which might worthily require a large treatise of itself), but to make way to show the beginning of this plantation, which is that I aim at." He also offers a general rationale for his procedures:

> I have been the larger in these things, and so shall crave leave in some like passages following (though in other things I shall labor to be more contract) that their children may see with what difficulties their fathers

wrestled in going through these things in their first beginnings. . . . As
also that some use may be made hereof in after times by others in such
like weighty employments.[7]

In making this claim for the utility—both retrospective and prospec-
tive—of his history, Bradford assumes that his material forms a whole,
bounded if not altogether complete, and that it is capable of taking a lasting shape. The second book, of course, can be understood as belying
these very assumptions.

Yet the qualitative shift from one part of the history to the other is not
quite as thoroughgoing as the evidence of designedness in the first book
and the lack of such evidence in the second would seem to indicate.
Bradford's method in the first book appears to fit the providential model
well in the sense that the "good form" and clear emplotment of the history reflects the form of God's plan for the Pilgrims; there is an implied
ratio between logical narrative and inevitable cosmic progression. On the
other hand, good form (as Hayden White has often argued)[8] is a common
feature of secular history as well, and it can be matched with other kinds
of progression besides the providential.

Even the historical accounts in the Bible, surely the authoritative text
for Bradford on matters of narrative as on most other matters, often lack
a strong providentialist impulse. There could hardly be a starker tonal
contrast in the Old Testament than between the relentless triumphalism
of the book of Joshua and the murky account of interethnic politics in the
book of Judges, though these two books together describe a continuous
period in the history of Canaan.[9] And the chronological long-marches of
the books of Kings and Chronicles do not reveal much sense of an over-
arching divine plan when read outside of a broader scriptural context.
This is to say that Bradford as a writer of providential history is not bound
by an ironclad definition of "the providential historian." There are sections in the first book—for instance, in the description of the practical
preparations for the journey to New England in chapters 5–7—that are as
mundane as any similar material in the second book. In these sections the
providentialist rhetoric largely disappears, though it may surface occasionally in the letters from John Robinson and other writers that Bradford
interpolates as part of the history.

Where such rhetoric reaches its highest pitch in the first book is, strikingly enough, in those parts of the narrative in which the Pilgrims are not transacting any business. Typically these parts involve embarking upon, being on board, or disembarking from a ship. When the community is literally at sea, its status as an economic entity is temporarily suspended until it reaches land once again. The fact of the community's isolation from its external relations, along with the sense of peril normally associated with ocean voyages in this period, provides Bradford with a kind of generic cue to intensify the theological and typological content of his account. This occurs in the description of the "fearful storm" that the first group of emigrants encountered on the way to Holland:

> But when man's hope and help wholly failed, the Lord's power and mercy appeared in their recovery. . . . When the water ran into their mouths and ears and the mariners cried out, "We sink, we sink!" they cried (if not with miraculous, yet with a great height or degree of divine faith), "Yet Lord Thou canst save! Yet Lord Thou canst save!" with such other expressions as I will forbear. Upon which the ship did not only recover, but shortly after the violence of the storm began to abate, and the Lord filled their afflicted minds with such comforts as everyone cannot understand, and in the end brought them to their desired haven.[10]

The familiar elements of providentialism are here: the reflection on the mystery of grace, the elevation of faith above works, the celebration of the efficacy of prayer, and the suggestion of a typological link with a scriptural event—in this case Christ's calming the wind and water while crossing the Sea of Galilee with the apostles, as recounted in all three of the synoptic Gospels (Matthew 8:23–27, Mark 4:35–41, Luke 8:22–25). But this is all in the context of a radical containment that is also—paradoxically, given the circumstances—a form of stasis: the Pilgrim community functions here as a simple and cohesive body, open to the ways of providence (or at least to those of providentialist interpretation), because on a foreign vessel in the middle of a difficult passage it can be very little else.

Similar moments occur in Bradford's account of the voyage to Cape Cod in chapter 9. There is the cautionary tale of the "very profane" and "haughty" sailor who paid dearly for mocking his land-loving passengers on the outward journey. "But it pleased God . . . to smite this young man with a grievous disease, of which he died in a desperate manner . . . and it was an astonishment to all his fellows for they noted it to be the just hand of God upon him." More significantly, there is the description of the arrival itself, where Bradford draws direct analogies to Paul's shipwreck on Malta in Acts 27 and Moses's vision of Canaan in Deuteronomy 3, and he goes so far as to substitute oceangoing "Englishmen" for Jacob's offspring in his paraphrase of two verses from Deuteronomy 26. This entire passage has been treated as an early interpretation of the American landscape and an illustration of English preconceptions about that landscape as "wilderness."[11]

What I want to stress about this passage, however, is that its typological density is closely aligned with the complete absence of a social milieu: "they had now no friends to welcome them nor inns to entertain or refresh their weatherbeaten bodies; no houses or much less towns to repair to, to seek for succor. . . . which way soever they turned their eyes (save upward to the heavens) they could have little solace or content in respect of any outward objects." The critical emphasis in this description has tended to fall on the "weatherbeaten face" and "wild and savage hue" of the country, but the lack of satisfactory "outward objects" is just as crucially the absence of friends, inns, houses, and towns—in other words, of the normal grounds for the transactions of daily life as the Pilgrims had known such life in England and Holland. The very last words of the first book point to the establishment of such grounds, "the first house for common use to receive them and their goods."[12]

These observations lead me to propose that the first book can best be treated as a case of "loose providentialism," as against a roughly contemporary Puritan history like Edward Johnson's *Wonder-Working Providence of Sions Saviour in New England* (published 1653), where providentialist patterning is consistently, indeed monotonously, apparent. Bradford's providentialist rhetoric is suited to occasions, particularly to originating events and periods of transition—to situations of genesis and exodus, as it were. As the Pilgrims settle into a way of life in what is now often termed a "contact zone," a world more like that portrayed in the book of Judges, these situations become fewer and fewer, to be replaced by instances of what Douglas Anderson describes as "Bradford's determination to hold in a kind of fruitful suspense the imputed relation between striking natural occurrences and providential design to which his contemporaries freely appealed."[13] Bradford neglects providentialist historiography in the second book not because of the perceived collapse of "the Pilgrim ideal" but because the generic appropriateness of providentialism to the material at hand is significantly diminished. This would imply as well that, early or late, *Of Plymouth Plantation* is not as tightly wedded to the forms of providential history as it is often thought to be.

Then what kind of history is Bradford trying to write? In his fine study of Bradford's relation to seventeenth-century print culture and practices of reading and writing, *William Bradford's Books,* Anderson suggests that the manuscript's historiographical character reflects quite a complex understanding of the precedents known to Bradford. In my reading, the answer to the question above is initially fairly simple: Bradford wants to write the genealogical history of a people from its first origins. Examples of such history, often dynastic in content and patriotic in theme, are manifold in the late medieval and early modern periods, drawing on both Greco-Roman and Judaeo-Christian influences and ranging along various points between the strictly providential and the strictly secular. Bradford might have had at least a passing acquaintance with the nationalistic chronicle histories of Edward Hall, Raphael Holinshed, and John Stow, all of which fall more toward the secular end.[14]

Such histories are structured by births, deaths, and inheritances, but the matter within the frame is chiefly occupied with the deeds of individuals, deeds that are inseparable from the identities of the persons who enact them and that are conceived as having a moral centrality, suffusing the history with whatever values the historian intends to promulgate. The very ancient notion of history as a narrative of particular deeds—generally *res gestae,* the deeds of monarchs, generals, or other types of "great men"—lends itself well to histories constructed upon simple, linear movement in a clearly defined direction: to accounts of long journeys to specific places of refuge or settlement, of the rise or decline of noble houses, of missions of conversion, of military campaigns such as the Crusades.[15]

This kind of movement appears to be characteristic of both universal history and chronicle, the two medieval models for historiography that Emory Elliott, in his survey of Puritan writing in New England in the first volume of the *Cambridge History of American Literature,* identifies as primary influences on Bradford's practice. Universal history, following Augustine's *De Civitate Dei,* may reveal a "larger pattern of God's plan in the recorded events," and chronicle may be "a straightforward account of narrative details," but neither requires complicated narrative strategies. In Elliott's view, the second book tells a familiar Old Testament story about "the deaths of the first-generation patriarchs, the spread of sin, and the weakening of the church" while still functioning in more mundane terms as "a practical man's sober accounting of the trials, pressures, and even fractures the colony had experienced."[16]

As far as Bradford's "intendment" goes, *Of Plymouth Plantation* is not especially distinctive and could sit easily with Elliott's description of its debts to both universal and chronicle history. What renders the book unusual is that, forced by the sheer pressure of the "matter" with which Bradford has to work, it moves rather rapidly outside of these traditional sorts of historiography. Bradford's history is distinguished from its putative models by its awareness of—and its willingness to consider, if sometimes quite reluctantly—the possibility that events are not unilaterally determined but have multiple causes, causes that cannot be accounted for satisfactorily by a recording of *res gestae* under either divine or temporal authority. In other words, Bradford, in *Of Plymouth Plantation,* is effectively moving beyond an understanding of history as a record of mere deeds (whether or not he considers those deeds to involve God's will and its manifestations) toward an understanding of history as an examination of a set of *relations,* many of which do not register in genealogical terms—or, for that matter, in the terms of "a straightforward account of narrative details." The project of the Pilgrims, while it could be categorized after a fashion as a journey, a mission, a campaign, or even the emergence (or decay) of a "family," resists being simplified into any one of these things alone, and one of the most salient categories—that of the business venture—rarely finds a place in the histories of Bradford's era.

Bradford is caught between the divergent requirements for writing genealogical history and what is now termed economic history, at a time when the requirements for the latter are largely invisible compared to the former. For example, Francis Bacon, in book 2 of *The Advancement of Learning,* divides history into four categories, "Natural, Civil, Ecclesiastical, and Literary." There is no obvious place in this scheme for historical accounts of commercial activity. Bacon does create a subcategory under natural history called "History of Nature Wrought or Mechanical," which would include agriculture and manual arts as two of its subjects, but he seems to have in mind nothing more abstract than a history of material technologies. The other possible niche for matters of business would be in one of the minor partitions under civil history, "Journals," which consider "accidents of a meaner nature."[17] That the historical dimension of commerce failed to impress itself on one of the greatest analytical minds of the era should help to indicate the extent of the problem faced by Bradford. Working from a fairly restricted palette of scriptural, classical, and ecclesiastical models for the task he has set himself, he wants to write a history of a community of like-minded believers that is at the same time, and just as significantly, the history of a joint-stock company embarked on a colonial business venture.

Yet Bradford's conception of the colonial polity—where the emphasis is on self-containment and the significant actions of the body's members—is at historiographical cross-purposes with his incipient understanding of the colonial business venture, where individuals' actions lose their particularity as they are fanned out onto the intricate web of commerce, and where the Pilgrims come into ambiguous contact with the other sorts of communities that fall within this same web. The microcosm of Plymouth Plantation cannot be stretched to fit smoothly over the macrocosm of the New England colonial economy. The hesitations, inconsistencies, and longueurs of the second book suggest Bradford's difficulty in superimposing one over the other. As a way of approaching this difficulty, I would like to offer "macrocosmic" readings of material from the second book concerning what I take to be two of its representative figures, Thomas Morton and Isaac Allerton. It should be said that Morton and Allerton are two figures among a number that might serve (John Oldham and James Sherley come to mind), but they do illustrate in reasonably compact fashion the broader trends of the second book.

Outsiders: Thomas Morton,
the Dutch, and Frontier Trade

The famous account of Morton's escapades in the annals for 1628 is generally read in terms of its contrasts with Morton's competing account of the same set of events in *New English Canaan*. But the Morton episode appears as part of a larger narrative in which Bradford seeks to explain a significant shift in the social and economic relations, particularly in the trade relations, prevailing in New England in the 1630s and 1640s.[18]

The crisis that requires an explanation involves, very literally, the empowerment of the Native Americans of Massachusetts by way of commerce with the colonists—an economic and, more troublesome still, a technological empowerment:

> Hitherto the Indians of these parts had no pieces nor other arms but their bows and arrows, nor of many years after; neither durst they scarce handle a gun, so much were they afraid of them. And the very sight of one (though out of kilter) was a terror unto them. But those Indians to the east parts, which had commerce with the French, got pieces of them, and they in the end made a common trade of it.

The rhetorical progression of the gun from a frightening symbol—a totem, as it were—representing the colonists' territorial power to a functional tool among the Native Americans appears here to originate in "commerce with the French" and "common trade." But "common trade," as Bradford is well aware, is not a closed system. The trade in firearms has other, more abstract causes—causes that, in the broad outlines of Bradford's account, implicate the Dutch from the south as well as the French from the "east." For in 1627 the Dutch introduced the manufacture and trade of wampum to the English and thence to the tribes of Massachusetts and northern New England, "and strange it was to see the great alteration it made in a few years among the Indians." Shell money, which had once had only limited use among the Narragansetts and Pequots, "grew thus to be a commodity in these parts" and "hath now continued . . . about this 20 years, and . . . may prove a drug in time."[19] Bradford falls readily here into the language of trade, employing a colloquial expression for slow-moving merchandise that remains a part of the merchant's lexicon to this day.

Among the stock the Dutch traded in 1627 to interested parties in New England was not only wampum itself but an education in its uses: "Neither did the English of this Plantation or any other in the land, till now that they had knowledge of it from the Dutch, so much as know what it was, much less that it was a commodity of that worth and value."[20] There is an implicit distinction in the passage between the utility of a particular commodity—a utility that Bradford treats as more or less a priori—and the knowledge that actually allows individuals and groups to make use of that commodity within the sphere of trade. Knowledge, in other words, becomes one valuable commodity among others. And in this passage Bradford introduces another party to the commerce in wampum: the English, who become the beneficiaries of Dutch expertise in this market, enabling them to enter the market themselves.

Here I need to digress for an interval to address Pilgrim attitudes toward the Dutch, since these attitudes figure significantly in Bradford's understanding of the Morton episode and help to determine the symbolic function of that episode within Bradford's history. While French traders from Canada could easily enough be categorized as direct political, economic, and even theological competitors with the English, the Dutch occupied a much more ambiguous position at the boundaries of the Pilgrims' community life, having traded many things (knowledge included) with Bradford's compatriots over a long period. Amsterdam and Leyden had provided the earliest havens for the Scrooby expatriates, who came over to the Netherlands on the prospect, as Bradford says, of "freedom of religion for all men."[21]

This freedom nonetheless had its threatening aspects. The unusually open character of the Dutch market (relative at least to its counterparts elsewhere in Europe) made for a distinctly polyglot environment in the Low Countries. Amsterdam housed an assortment of political, religious, and economic immigrants from many different places, including a significant number of Jews. Leyden, as home to one of the most prestigious—and liberal—universities in Europe, had a diverse population, with students coming from as far away as Russia. An anonymous English satirist of the 1660s linked Dutch prosperity to this peculiar diversity: "They countenance only Calvinism, but for Trades sake they Tolerate all others, except the Papists; which is the reason why the treasure and stock of most Nations is transported thither, where there is full Liberty of Conscience: you may be what the Devil you will there, so you be but peaceable." Bradford vividly describes the disorienting effect of Dutch cultural life on the Pilgrim settlers: "they heard a strange and uncouth language, and beheld the different manners and customs of the people, with their strange fashions and attires; all so far differing from that of their plain country villages (wherein they were bred and had so long lived) as it seemed they were come into a new world."[22] The explicit contrast here is between the exotic pluralism of the Netherlands and the communal stability of "plain country villages," villages that Bradford renders as both centers of origin and emblems of continuity for the Pilgrims—"wherein they were bred and had so long lived."

One of the subtle historical ironies of the Pilgrims' arrival in the other "new world" across the Atlantic is that the milieu that prompted their departure from Europe soon reappeared in a recognizably similar form in North America. New Netherland was an unsuccessful and relatively short-lived colonial experiment, yet its influence reached northward and certainly touched the Plymouth settlers, for from an early point New Netherland displayed a diversity not unlike what the Pilgrims would have remembered in Amsterdam and Leyden. Twenty years after the colony was first settled, the Jesuit Isaac Jogues (perhaps exaggerating) noted that eighteen languages were spoken there. The linguistic mélange had its religious counterpart. In 1655 the conservative Dutch Reformed minister Johannes Megapolensis complained that "we have here Papists, Mennonites and Lutherans among the Dutch; also many Puritans or Independents, and many Atheists and various other servants of Baal among the English under this Government, who conceal themselves under the name of Christians." He went on to inveigh against Jews, some of whom had already settled in New Netherland (by way of Brazil!) the previous year. The colony also contained more than a few freed slaves, thanks to the absence there of racially discriminatory laws, as well as the West India Company's unusually lax regulation of the slave trade.[23]

Given their tolerance for the plural and the polyglot in their social affairs, the Dutch in their renewed proximity presented the Pilgrims with complexities that may have been familiar from past experience but remained difficult to untangle. The nature of the dynamic is quietly suggested by an exchange of formal correspondence from 1627 that Bradford includes in his narrative. The first letter is addressed to Bradford from Isaack de Rasieres, secretary to the Council of New Netherland. De Rasieres, citing common interests (namely "our common enemy the Spaniards"), asks for an opportunity to trade with Plymouth: "if it so fall out that any good that come to our hands from our native country may be serviceable to you, we shall take ourselves bound to help and accommodate you therewith, either for beaver or any other wares or merchandise that you should be pleased to deal for." If the Pilgrims do not wish to buy, perhaps they will be willing to sell "beaver or otter or such like commodities as may be useful to us." In his reply Bradford cites the alliance of the English and Dutch against Spain as "sufficient to unite us together in love and good neighborhood in all our dealings" and expresses gratitude for "the good and courteous entreaty we have found in your country, having lived there many years with freedom and good content." Bradford claims that De Rasieres's offer "is to us very acceptable, and we doubt not but in short time we may have profitable commerce and trade together." He then goes on, however, to demur firmly, if politely: "But for this year we are fully supplied with all necessaries, both for clothing and other things. But hereafter it is like we shall deal with you if your rates be reasonable." The notion of "good neighborhood" here seems to involve maintaining a respectful distance from one's neighbors.[24]

From Bradford's point of view there were excellent reasons for keeping the Dutch at arm's length, in spite of any felt obligations to the Pilgrims' former "hosts." New Netherland might offer to the Pilgrims (just as the "old" Netherlands had) the potential, at least, for participation in a productive mercantile network; at the same time, it offered near at hand an antithetical, if in some ways tantalizing, model of what a colonial community could be: an *economic* body, paradoxically disembodied, active but nebulous and contradictory, full of life but always verging on chaos—"a Babel of Confusion," as Megapolensis believed it was becoming.[25]

Such a body was perceived, at least, to have a dangerous talent for assimilating and dissolving within itself the identity of other bodies, including the identity of the plain country village of like-minded believers that Bradford at one level imagined Plymouth Colony to be. The danger of dissolution, portrayed in the familiar terms of a "generation gap," figures prominently in Bradford's account of "the Reasons and Causes of . . . [the Pilgrims'] Removal" to New England:

> But that which was more lamentable . . . was that many of their children . . . were drawn away by evil examples and dangerous courses, get-

ting the reins off their necks and departing from their parents. Some became soldiers, others took upon them far voyages by sea, and others
some worse courses tending to dissoluteness and the danger of their
souls, to the great grief of their parents and dishonor of God. So that
they saw their posterity would be in danger to degenerate and be cor-
rupted.[26]

Here personal "dissoluteness" and communal dissolution are readily
conflated; Bradford locates the cause of this particular problem both in
the general waywardness of youth *and* in the economic pressures of the
Pilgrims' Dutch environment—pressures that forced the newest members of the body outward to fend for themselves.

The Tower of Babel is the last monument that Bradford would want
erected in the environs of Massachusetts Bay, yet the second book often
suggests that such a tower is already built up to a point that invites divine
intervention—that New England is on the verge of a violent cosmopoli-
tanism based on trade, in which various "speakers" struggle (and usually
fail) to rise above the hubbub in order to establish a lingua franca (or a
common currency) for the entire region. The wampum trade itself offers
a compact illustration of the emerging state of affairs: the primary consequence of the development of this market is that, Bradford says, "it makes
the Indians of these parts rich and powerful and also proud thereby, and
fills them with pieces, powder and shot, which no laws can restrain."[27]
The sentence is built upon a nice parallelism between "rich"/"powerful"/"proud" and "pieces"/"powder"/"shot" (with the parallelism rein-
forced by a partial rhyme in the middle terms), which allows Bradford to
suggest a close relationship between the trade in wampum and the trade
in guns.

Bradford also implies here the working out of a clear causal sequence,
but one that moves in an interesting direction: wampum makes one
wealthy, wealth makes one powerful, power makes one proud—and pride
makes one enter into further commerce. The lack of "restraint" here re-
lates not to the Native Americans but to the "pieces, powder, and shot,"
and by extension to the trade in those goods, a trade enabled by "the baseness of sundry unworthy persons, both English, Dutch and French."[28]
This cause is also a consequence: trade, whether in wampum or guns, dissolves the distinctions between these national groups into a general cate-

gory of "baseness," a category that seems to involve class as much as it does moral standards. The vanguard of baseness as far as the English are concerned is represented for Bradford by the ever-suspect fishermen, participants in a commercial enterprise in which the markers of class and national origin had not been observed with much rigor for many years.

The discussion then turns to Morton, and the reader's initial impression may be that Bradford, having addressed the emergence of the Dutch as trading partners in New England, has now moved on to other matters of concern in the year 1628. But there is no actual break in the historical narrative; Bradford continues to trace the issue of Native American trade in guns back to what he views—perhaps with more conviction than accuracy—as its source. The section on Morton begins retrospectively: "About some three or four years before this time . . ." There is nothing very portentous about Morton's arrival in the country in the company of one Captain Wollaston (whom Bradford describes rather cryptically as "a man of pretty parts"). Other than having pretensions to being a colonial projector in his own right, with "some small adventure of his own or other men's amongst them," Morton's main distinction is his character as an untouchable, so to speak, unable to maintain the perquisites of class: he "had little respect among them [i.e., his fellow planters], and was slighted by the meanest servants." What enables Morton to begin to cut a figure in New England is a decision based, again, on commercial interests; Wollaston and company, "not finding things to answer their expectations nor profit to arise as they looked for," decamp for Virginia, where Wollaston finds a better trade—this time in human labor. He markets his servants "at good rates, selling their time to other men."[29] Morton gains his opportunity among those of Wollaston's group who remain behind, under the apparently ineffectual stewardship of Lieutenant Fitcher.

The critical emphasis at this point tends to fall on Morton, the "Lord of Misrule" with his "School of Atheism," as either a carnivalesque or a demonic figure, depending on one's point of view. All the drinking, dancing, and frisking that goes on at Mount Dagon, however, should not obscure the fact that Bradford presents Morton as a businessman whose first saleable commodity, other than "strong drink and other junkets," happens to be the "good counsel" he says he can provide to Wollaston's men. The counsel, as Bradford imagines Morton offering it, is in effect a pro-

posal to form a corporation: "'I, having a part in the Plantation, will receive you as my partners and consociates; so you may be free from service, and we will converse, plant, trade, and live together as equals and
support and protect one another.'"[30]

This is less the prospect of Utopia than of a joint-stock company that
does not limit its subscription to the upper classes. The democratic thrust
of the agreement, a kind of parody of the Mayflower Compact ("[We] . . .
solemnly and mutually in the presence of God and one of another,
Covenant and Combine ourselves together into a Civil Body Politic, for
our better ordering and preservation and furtherance of the ends afore-
said"), is particularly vexing to Bradford, who remarks later that settlers in
the vicinity "saw that they should keep no servants, for Morton would entertain any, how vile soever, and all the scum of the country or any dis-
contents would flock to him from all places, if this nest were not broken."
Mount Wollaston becomes Ma-re Mount, with all its attendant amuse-
ments, only after Morton and his new partners "had got some goods into
their hands, and got much by trading with the Indians." One of Bradford's
chief complaints against Morton is that this trade leads to scandalously
lavish expenditure on the wrong sort of commodities: "both wine and
strong waters in great excess (and, as some reported) £10 worth in a
morning." Bradford then describes Morton as making a momentous—in
Bradford's view, a catastrophic—business decision to avoid running his
operation into the red: "Now to maintain this riotous prodigality and pro-
fuse excess, Morton, thinking himself lawless, and hearing what gain the
French and fishermen made by trading of pieces, powder and shot to the
Indians, he as the head of this consortship began the practice of the same
in these parts."[31]

Bradford is careful to state that Morton's decision, made in his role "as
the head of this consortship," represents, so to speak, a corporate goal.
Yet Morton contributes a very individual sort of initiative to the new
trade: once again knowledge surfaces as among the most valuable of
commodities. "And first he taught . . . [the Indians] how to use . . . [the
guns], to charge and discharge, and what proportion of powder to give
the piece, according to the size or bigness of the same; and what shot to
use for fowl and what for deer." The Native Americans subsequently become part of Morton's corporation as well: "having thus instructed them,

he employed some of them to hunt and fowl for him, so as they became far more active in that employment than any of the English." As in the case of those other formerly innocent knowers, Adam and Eve, their eyes are opened: "when they saw the execution that a piece would do, and the benefit that might come by the same, they became mad (as it were) after them and would not stick to give any price they could attain for them; accounting their bows and arrows but baubles in comparison of them."[32] Bradford's narrative proceeds by way of reversals: as the once nondescript Morton becomes a figure to be reckoned with, so the Native Americans come to view their once formidable weapons as "baubles"—a word, interestingly enough, used quite often by seventeenth-century colonists to describe the kinds of items they liked to trade with the "savages."

Now one might say that knowledge is the devil's stock in trade, and Bradford goes some distance to portray Morton as the original sinner in this particular ordeal: "here I may take occasion to bewail the mischief that this wicked man began in these parts, and which since, base covetousness prevailing in men that should *know* better, has now at length got the upper hand and made this thing common, notwithstanding any laws to the contrary."[33] Morton's trading post was so small and its range of influence so limited that this passage may well register as hyperbole in its conspicuous effort to attribute the responsibility for a large-scale crisis to one individual; the reader is aware that the narrative possesses a certain allegorical force here above its factual content. Yet there are aspects of Bradford's account that forestall its interpretation as a New England version of the third chapter of Genesis with Morton figuring as the serpent in a New World Eden, and these relate to the commercial character of Morton's activity.

Here it may be necessary to distinguish in a rough-and-ready way between Bradford as a storyteller and Bradford as an explicator, with the very specific sense in the latter case of someone who unfolds things, and, secondarily, develops or expands them—one who teases out the strands to render something upon a larger field. Another way of thinking about the explicator's activity would be in terms of what the philosopher William Walsh called "colligation." Walsh applied this term, borrowed from the nineteenth-century Cambridge philosopher William Whewell, to a common mode of historical explanation:

> when asked to explain a particular event . . . [historians] will begin by
> tracing connections between that event and others with which it stands
> in inner relationship. . . . The underlying assumption here is that differ-
> ent historical events can be regarded as going together to constitute a
> single process, a whole of which they are all parts and in which they be-
> long together in a specially intimate way. And the first aim of the histo-
> rian, when he is asked to explain some event or other, is to see it as part
> of such a process, to locate it in its context by mentioning other events
> with which it is bound up.[34]

With its emphasis on relationships and the analysis of relationships, colligation as a "style" of historiography is thus not limited by the conventions of linear narrative; a pure "colligator" would not necessarily be a storyteller, at least not in any simple sense of telling a story.

In Bradford's case both the role of storyteller and that of explicator/ colligator are proper to his activity as a historian; indeed the two roles overlap, but they also reflect rather different generic requirements. As a storyteller, Bradford aims for a simplicity of effect and employs limited means to achieve that effect: a small cast of characters, a linear plot, an obvious goal to be reached. The "story" of Morton is one of a wicked man, a tempter, who disrupts the prevailing order of the community and is suitably punished by the forces of good, represented by Captain Standish. But this story is in turn embedded in an explication of a complex phenomenon that resists being broken down and reassembled with the familiar tools of the storyteller. Bradford's account of the arming of the New England tribes moves on multiple planes, and the relations between those planes are not always clear.

A consequence of this is that the account takes on the quality that A. P. Rossiter, in several of his great lectures on Shakespeare, called "two-eyedness." The reader perceives an oscillation between the perspective of the story, where Morton is unquestionably the primary source of the problem, and the perspective of the explication, where Morton is merely an agent in a lengthy causal chain that neither begins nor ends with him. Rather than attempt further, by way of explanation, to sort out Morton's actual responsibility for a disturbing state of affairs, Bradford concludes the account by reverting to storytelling, with the comical episode of the siege of Ma-re Mount and Morton's blustering defense and (nearly) bloodless defeat. Bradford then bids farewell to the entire matter: "I have been too long about so unworthy a person, and bad a cause."[35]

Yet the shadow of this "bad cause" extends beyond the shadow cast by the "unworthy person" and involves actors who do not fit readily into the story, about whom Bradford speaks with difficulty. These actors are shadowy presences in Bradford's commentary on the current state of the arms trade in New England:

> in a time of war or danger, as experience hath manifested, . . . when lead hath been scarce and men for their own defense would gladly have given a groat a pound . . . yet hath it been bought up and sent to other places and sold to such as trade it with the Indians at 12*d* the pound. And it is like they give 3*s* or 4*s* the pound, for they will have it at any rate. And these things have been done in the same times when some of their neighbors and friends are daily killed by the Indians, or are in danger thereof and live but at the Indians' mercy. Yea some, as they have acquainted them with all other things, have told them how gunpowder is made, and all the materials in it, and they are to be had in their own land; and I am confident, could they attain to make saltpeter, they would teach them to make powder.[36]

The passage presents the reader with a thicket of passive constructions and ungrounded pronouns. The lead for shot "hath . . . been bought up and sent . . . and sold"; "these things have been done." The culprits are "such" and "some." Not buyers, senders, sellers, nor traders assume a specific identity, though Bradford implies that the activity is *seriatim* and involves more than a few hands. The use of "they" and "their" is ambiguous throughout; in the last sentence it seems to apply alternately to "some," to materials for gunpowder, and to the Native Americans (or possibly back to "some" again). The meaning of "them," however, is straightforward; it always refers to "the Indians," who are, after all, the ones at the receiving end. This referential trauma in Bradford's prose occurs because commerce, and the participation in commerce, has collapsed the boundary between the Pilgrim community at Plymouth and "such as trade . . . with the Indians." The passage erases distinctions between one community and another, suggesting the inescapably porous character of trading relations in New England. Here as elsewhere, knowledge is a significant commodity: before the Native Americans can produce gunpowder of their own, "some" must "teach" them. A difficult question bubbles to the surface of this strangely anonymous melting pot: *who* knows? Bradford evokes a cloud of witnesses but is not prepared to single out any one of them. While Morton may be presented as a literal scapegoat, one whose expulsion has a corrective or cathartic effect on the community at large, the account raises the prospect of agents other than Morton moving about on the periphery of Ma-re Mount, perhaps even in the heart of Plymouth itself.

Insiders: Isaac Allerton and Plymouth's Debts

As a piece of historical reconstruction, the Morton episode reveals a conceptual discomfort that appears in many other places in the second book, most noticeably in Bradford's lengthy efforts to make sense of Allerton's behavior as agent for the colony in England. It should be said that Bradford is under no illusions about Allerton, making him the butt of much proverbial and scriptural wisdom about the dangers of seeking after riches at the hazard of one's soul.[37] In many ways, Allerton, even more than Morton, emerges as the archvillain of the history, disastrously compromising the colony's finances while stubbornly pursuing "his own particular" and "private benefit." Bradford recalls that it was in fact Allerton who "for base gain" brought Morton *back* to the colony from England after the first expulsion, using him "as a scribe" until he was forced "to pack him away," largely due to Morton's propensity for trading guns with Native Americans.[38] This is only one of many sorts of malfeasance on Allerton's part that preoccupy Bradford throughout the annals from 1628 to 1633.

Yet Bradford also shows a deep and initially puzzling reluctance to condemn Allerton absolutely, despite the extensive (and extensively recorded) damage he does to the plantation's interests: "though private gain I do persuade myself was some cause to lead Mr. Allerton aside in these beginnings; yet I think or at least charity carries me to hope, that he intended to deal faithfully with them [the Pilgrims] in the main." This is a severely qualified form of excuse, but it does suggest the nature of the problem: while Morton can be readily demonized, Allerton cannot. As the commentators to the Massachusetts Historical Society edition tactfully note, "Bradford has on the whole dealt kindly with one who seems to have been unsuccessful in all his ventures."[39]

Some of the reasons for this forbearance require no great detective work. For instance, Bradford had close personal and administrative connections with Allerton that rarely emerge in the text. In the annal for 1621, Bradford does describe (in the third person) his election as governor: "and [Bradford] being not recovered of his illness, in which he had been near the point of death, Isaac Allerton was chosen to be an assistant unto him who, by renewed election every year, continued sundry years together. Which I here note once for all."[40] In fact, Bradford never again refers to Allerton as his assistant. He implies here that had he not been so ill he would never have needed an assistant at all; it was other members of the community who kept electing Allerton to the position. Allerton had also become the son-in-law of William Brewster, one of the most respected members of the colony. Both of these facts point to what probably weighs most heavily on Bradford's account of the man: Allerton, passenger on the *Mayflower* and signer of the Compact, is a member of the Pilgrim community in a way that Morton never could be. It is possible to see Bradford's ambivalence about Allerton resulting from conflict of interest, from the common tendency to "forgive one's own," or even from an attempt to maintain a Christlike tolerance of the individual sinner.

In terms of Bradford's effort to write history, however, the ambivalence appears to spring from his difficulty in placing Allerton appropriately in the narrative of Plymouth's fortunes. Allerton's situation in this regard is close to the reverse of Morton's. Where Morton becomes a personification of the dangerously porous boundary between the community and the outer world, Allerton is very much *in medias res*. The majority of his transactions are not with Dutch, French, or native outsiders but with the colonists and their backers in England. He is, in other words, a significant representative of the Pilgrim community *as* a community. At the same time, he is a source of confusion not only to Plymouth but also to Bradford in his chosen role as historian of the colony. Noting Allerton's ultimate discharge as Plymouth's agent in the annal for 1630, Bradford continues, "But these businesses were not ended till many years after, nor well understood of a long time, but folded up in obscurity and kept in the clouds, to the great loss and vexation of the Plantation, who in the end were (for peace sake) forced to bear the unjust burden of them, to their almost undoing. As will appear if God give life to finish this history."[41]

This last sentence finds Bradford mindful of a story to be told, indeed to be completed. But what kind of story? Often the "accounting" in the annals concerning Allerton is less of *res gestae* than of monies disbursed, received, loaned, repaid, lost. The climax of this narrative, as it were, occurs in the annal for 1631, when Bradford turns to Allerton's actual accounts: "They were so large and intricate as they [the Plymouth examiners] could not well understand them, much less examine and correct them without a great deal of time and help and his own presence, which was now hard to get amongst them. And it was two or three years before they could bring them to any good pass, but never make them perfect." This serves as a précis of the historiographical problem that Allerton presents: his narrative, like his accounts, can never be made "perfect," can never be fully sorted out. Bradford does make gestures at bringing Allerton's history to closure along providential lines, showing how "God crossed him mightily" in his later ventures and how he was "called to account for these and other his gross miscarriages" by the Plymouth church: "He confessed his fault and promised better walking, and that he would wind himself out of these courses so soon as he could, etc." But Allerton—as Bradford's wry "etc." implies—keeps surfacing as a nuisance and distraction for several more pages, until he abruptly fades away as an active participant in the history of Plymouth when Bradford says, near the beginning of the annal for 1633, "I leave these matters and come to other things."[42]

The Allerton material is likely to be vexing for the present-day reader, not only because Allerton himself is portrayed so colorlessly—Bradford manages to make Morton more vivid in a few pages than he makes Allerton over the course of several annals—but also because of the general abstractness of this part of the narrative. The two trading-cum-fishing ships that become the vehicles for many of Allerton's financial machinations, the inauspiciously named *Friendship* and *White Angel*, figure almost as prominently as "characters" as do regularly mentioned individuals like Allerton, Edward Winslow, Sherley, or Timothy Hatherley. This abstract quality makes better sense, however, if it is understood as reflecting

Bradford's uncertainty about attributing responsibility for the extraordinarily messy crisis of indebtedness among the Pilgrims during the early 1630s. Allerton is, after all, mainly a functionary of the colony, following (albeit often in a very distorted form) the instructions of his colleagues at Plymouth and in London. In a telling passage from the annal for 1629, Bradford recounts Allerton's purchase on the colony's account of a large quantity of salt from a fishing station at a good price: "And shortly after he might have had £30 clear profit for it, without any more trouble about it." But a group led by Winslow "stayed him from selling the salt" with the idea, apparently improvised on the spot, that they could contract at Bristol or elsewhere for a fishing ship and lade it with merchandise rather than salt, given that they now had a supply of salt on hand that the fisherman could use for preserving their catch once the ship made port in New England. "And so they might have a full supply of goods without paying freight, and in due season, which might turn greatly to their advantage." The only objection to this scheme came from Bradford himself, "who had no mind to it, seeing they had always lost by fishing"; but even he, "seeing their earnestness, . . . gave way."[43]

The responsibility for what Bradford obviously views as a harebrained scheme is fairly well distributed here, even though Allerton, by buying the salt in the first place, is in some fashion the "cause."[44] Allerton's deeds provide Bradford with a way of outlining dimensions of collective activity at Plymouth for which Bradford's historiographical vocabulary lends him no very precise descriptive terms and that cannot be subsumed under the metaphor of the community as a simple, self-contained body going about its individual "business." It is not that Bradford elides the personal contribution of Allerton, or anyone else, to Plymouth's financial quandary. But what concerns him most, and what he struggles to illuminate, is the dynamic and overdetermined economic life of the colony, dense with multiple and competing interests as well as uncontrollable elements (weather, costs of shipping, seasonal variations in price, supply and demand, and so on) that Bradford generally neglects to assign to the workings of Providence. He can afford to be relatively light-handed in his treatment of Allerton because it is not the man himself but his *accounts* that matter in the history of Plymouth. His significance lies, for instance, in the £113 expended on the salt and the loss of £30 of easy profit, since the expense and profit belong to the community and help to form an index of its successes and failures.

Like Morton, Allerton is a character who invites "two-eyedness" across the divide between storytelling and explication, though the emphases fall rather differently in the Allerton sequences than they do in the Morton episode. Bradford seems aware throughout these sequences that explication (analysis, that is, of the complex conditions that lead to specific economic consequences for the colony) is the most important historical task before him, but up to a point he continues to rely on the old familiar tools of history understood as stories about the deeds of prominent men—up to a point. Bradford's reconstruction of events gradually moves away from such stories toward a stress on the data in the financial records of the colony, data that prove to be more useful in dealing with the historical problems raised by the Pilgrims' fiscal crisis in the early 1630s. At some level, Bradford recognizes that the numbers tell the story.

A New History?

As I have suggested earlier in this chapter, the experience of reading *Of Plymouth Plantation* becomes less troublesome if one thinks of Bradford as moving not so much away from one kind of history as toward another. The movement is tentative because this other kind of history is still so ill defined in the seventeenth century and is one that Bradford writes almost in spite of himself. The impulse is always present to transform Plymouth into a closed community, a simulacrum of John Robinson's primal flock, whose "outside relations" are mainly typological and turned toward the past. Yet Bradford remains mindful at the same time of the fact that the colony is an adventure, that its supporters in London are looking to the "books" with other ideas in mind, that the Pilgrims have competitors (Dutch, French, Native Americans, Bay Colonists, and fishermen), and that the project is necessarily an open-ended one, faced toward a future where the years succeed one another in the normal way but never turn out to mean precisely the same thing. In other words, Bradford confronts as both an obstacle and an obligation what over the last three centuries has become a commonplace: the notion that human events have an economic context.

Is Bradford one of the first economic historians? To answer this question affirmatively may seem unduly bold, until one considers how few histories of the period are actually *like* Bradford's. Perhaps the closest thematic analog is Richard Hakluyt the Younger's *The Principall Navigations, Voiages and Discoveries of the English Nation,* first published in 1589, greatly expanded in the second edition of 1598–1600, and continued to massive proportions in the seventeenth century by Samuel Purchas under the title *Purchas his Pilgrimes.* Richard Helgerson has argued that the novelty of the *Principall Navigations* lies in Hakluyt's treatment of merchants as significant, even heroic, actors in English history and his placement of commerce at the center of English national life.[45] Hakluyt's magnum opus is not, strictly speaking, a historical narrative; it is instead an anthology that contains narratives along with many other kinds of documents. It would also be difficult to say with certainty that Hakluyt's work influenced Bradford's project in any way. Even so, there is a connection to be drawn between Hakluyt and Bradford, for both the *Principall Navigations* and *Of Plymouth Plantation* form part of the descriptive literature of English colonial expansion at its beginnings. It may be that, as Helgerson has claimed in Hakluyt's case, the sheer necessity of commercial activity to the process of colonization forces economic concerns into prominence in Bradford's narrative in a way that might not otherwise occur if he were simply writing "domestic" history.

In any event, this sort of problem cannot be raised satisfactorily if Bradford's work is simply assigned to the circumscribed region of providentialist history. I have tried to suggest at different points in this chapter that, like the other texts I discuss in this book, *Of Plymouth Plantation* presents generic affiliations that range fairly widely and sometimes lead in unusual directions. This is not to say that Bradford *means* to be unusual. He seems to accept the role of a historian of economic contexts only grudgingly, because he recognizes how damaging such history is to his commemoration of the interior life of his community, and how distant he is from the hermetic self-assurance of, say, the author of the book of Joshua, or John Foxe in the *Acts and Monuments.* Yet one might also say that Bradford seems to relax into this strange role during the long course of writing his history, to find a way of writing commensurate with the matters that have pressed upon his memory and his conscience. The "incompleteness" of the second book of *Plymouth Plantation* has less to do with Bradford's final gesture of resignation over the failure of the Pilgrim dream than with his recognition that the history he is attempting to write has no real ending, because it is no longer the history of a body that either clearly lives or clearly dies. The second book is testimony to the difficulty of serving two masters—not only God and Mammon, but God and Clio.

3

—៣—

Importing the Metropolis

The Poetics of Urbanity in Thomas
Morton's *New English Canaan*

On the one hand, the sombre religious settlement; on the other, the
noisy trading-post,—two germs of civilized life in that immeasurable
wilderness, unbroken, save at Merry-Mount and Plymouth, from the
Penobscot to the Hudson. Yet that wilderness, though immeasurable to
them, was not large enough for both.

—CHARLES FRANCIS ADAMS,
Three Episodes of Massachusetts History

This man arrived in those parts, and hearing news of a Town that was
much praised, he was desirous to go thither, and see how things stood;
where his entertainment was their best, I dare be bold to say; for, although they had but 3. Cows in all, yet had they fresh butter and a sal-
let of eggs in dainty wise, a dish not common in a wilderness.

—THOMAS MORTON, *New English Canaan*

Even by the standards of the other texts that I am examining here,
with their mystifying principles of organization and sometimes
opaque intentions, Thomas Morton's *New English Canaan* stands out as an
oddity—in Thomas Cartelli's words, "a minority report . . . on New World
promise and possibilities," and according to John Seelye, "a bacchanalian
car filled with joyous, pagan plenty," but also, as Daniel Shea has described it, "an evolutionary relic and dead end, clumsy-winged, perverse
even in its flights."[1] A promotional tract that grades bewilderingly into

recondite satire of Morton's enemies at Plymouth and Salem, larded with high-flown but sometimes incomprehensible verse, the book is a case study in poor communication. Its appeal to the Laudian establishment to exercise more control over the Puritans in New England had no impact that can be documented from the historical record; as Charles Francis Adams Jr. noted in his 1883 edition of *New English Canaan* (until recently the only "modern" edition of the book), "It does not appear . . . that at the time it attracted any general or considerable notice in America; while in England, of course, it would have interested only a small class of persons." Adams—son and namesake of Abraham Lincoln's minister to Great Britain, elder brother of the formidable Henry, grandson of John Quincy, great-grandson of John, and a distinguished representative of old-line Bay culture in his own right—was by no means a disinterested judge of Morton, given his family's long and prominent residence in the immediate vicinity of Morton's former outpost, but he forcefully captured the difficulties that Morton's writing presents:

> it is amazing how a man who knew as much as Morton knew of events and places now full of interest, could have sat down to write about them at all, and then, after writing so much, have told so little. Rarely stating anything quite correctly—the most careless and slipshod of authors,—he took positive pleasure in concealing what he meant to say under a cloud of metaphor. Accordingly, when printed, the *New Canaan* fell still-born from the press.[2]

In his own lifetime, Morton's public success, as such, was in vexing men like William Bradford, John Endicott, and John Winthrop, and in getting himself thrown out of the colony. It was not achieved as an author.

Despite its minuscule impact in the seventeenth century, *New English Canaan* continues to attract scholarly interest as one of the most direct expressions of dissent from the "New England Way" to appear in print in the early colonial period. Morton is primarily famous for the travesty of his fractious relations with the Plymouth Colony in the third book; the account in chapters 14 and 15 of the May Day revels at Ma-re Mount and Morton's subsequent "battle" with Captain Shrimp and the Nine Worthies (also known as Myles Standish and his allies) is much anthologized, usually in conjunction with Bradford's very different reading of the same sequence of events in *Of Plymouth Plantation*.[3] The conflict between Morton's and

Bradford's perspectives on events in the late 1620s has, of course, been the main focus for the relatively small number of scholars and critics who have tried to make sense of *New English Canaan*. Morton's book is historically valuable as, at the least, a colorful riposte to the dominant Pilgrim/Puritan narrative of colonization in Massachusetts—and perhaps it would be fine to stop there, given the book's highly erratic readability. I believe, though, that it is worth inquiring into other concerns that might be concealed in Morton's "cloud of metaphor," for at bottom, *New English Canaan* is yet another example of an "advertisement" for New England, and the question of what Morton meant to advertise (other than the follies and excesses of the colonial Puritan polity) still hovers around the text.

In this chapter, then, I want to consider Morton's knowledge project in *New English Canaan* in light of a familiar topic in the history of such colonial advertisement, but one whose inner dimensions continue to bear further examination: the matter of the habitability of the New World for European settlers. Much of the promotional literature associated with New England can be understood to emerge from the need to refute the charge, or at least the anxiety, that the land is unsuitable for colonization, that it is, as Bradford described it in *Of Plymouth Plantation* in his account of the first landing, "a hideous and desolate wilderness, full of wild beasts and wild men."[4] Bradford's history is, of course, itself a refutation of the argument against habitability. The promotional texts gradually shift from offering counterarguments to presenting testimony that a viable civil life is possible in North America. One of Morton's own early claims in *New English Canaan* is that "this Country of new England is by all judicious men accounted the principal part of all America for habitation and the commodiousness of the Sea."[5] Soon enough in the history of the English colonies, habitability is no longer a subject of debate; it is confirmed by the obvious progress of the colonists in becoming permanent inhabitants.

The problem then assumes another form, prefaced not by "whether" but by "how" and "what." Given a livable place, how should the colonists go about living in it? What kind of habitation is appropriate to the setting and the settlers? This problem, one might say, is worked out at ground level; the solutions are evident in the archaeological remains of villages, towns, forts, and farms throughout the colonies, as well as in a documentary record of plats, land transactions, municipal ordinances, and so on.

The texts from the early period also offer abundant indications of concern about the nature of New World settlement—about population density, employment, transportation, trade, local and regional government, relations with indigenous peoples, and the use and abuse of natural resources. Moreover, these texts provide evidence of a relatively elusive element in the evolution of colonial habitation, one that is not so easy to identify in the material record of town plans and old foundation lines: a debate over what I will call the "style" of settlement.

I use the term *style,* as opposed to *ideology, program,* or *concept,* since what I am trying to isolate here is roughly akin to style in a novel, painting, or other work of art:[6] style, that is, as a sum of various features (not all of them introduced deliberately or self-consciously) that serves to differentiate one made thing from another; moreover, style as a form of discourse, one that expresses the complex and dynamic relationships between and within different media, as well as between those media and the motives leading to their application. The peculiarity of a style, then, lies in the peculiarity of its combination of elements. In this sense, many parts of the human world—persons, families, institutions, landscapes, buildings, cuisines, and so on—display styles. It is routine, for example, to refer to cities, towns, and regions as having distinct styles that separate them from counterparts with many superficial similarities: Boston and Providence, Nantucket and Edgartown, Vermont and New Hampshire—the pairings are apt in many ways, yet in each pair one place is very unlikely to be mistaken for the other in terms of style. A high value, sometimes even a moral or spiritual value, attaches to style because it is such a convenient (if not always an entirely accurate) marker of identity. Thus there are, throughout history and at every level of human activity, continuous efforts to define, preserve, manipulate, and manufacture all manner of styles.

While the early colonists in New England find few if any applications for the actual word *style* in their writings, they are as concerned about the style(s) of their habitation as they are about its other aspects. They think of their settlements not only as being ordered around particular social, religious, and economic priorities, but also as having a tone, an ambience, and a characteristic demeanor—as having a personality as well as a mind or a body. When Winthrop famously speaks of the city on a hill in his lay sermon "A Modell of Christian Charity," he invokes Christ's authority as expressed in the fifth chapter of Matthew, as well as a more abstract spiritual ideal; yet he also pictures a particular kind of city, literally a "capital" with its head prominently above its surroundings, exemplary in the style of Jerusalem or Rome or Athens, so that "the eyes of all people are upon us."[7] In the event, the settlers at Shawmut, soon to be named Boston, would take relatively little practical advantage of the ridge (with Beacon Hill as its summit) that formed the high ground on the narrow peninsula where they decided to establish their city. But Winthrop's sermon at least hints of an aspiration toward, a projection of, a city characterized by *elevation* in both physical and metaphysical ways.

In *New English Canaan*, Morton also imagines a city on a hill, though not quite so lofty as the one imagined by Winthrop. (Morton's own place of settlement was on the summit of a low coastal hill at Passonagessit, in what is now the town of Quincy; it came to be called Mount Wollaston after the name of the leader of the colonizing party in which Morton arrived).[8] This "city" is more like London than Jerusalem, in that commerce rather than worship is its explicit motive force. It centers, like Winthrop's, around a kind of meetinghouse, but one that is public in ways that Winthrop and his fellow citizens would not accept. It is a place where settlers and Native Americans mingle without undue tension or discomfort, and where people talk, think, and act—and, significantly, write poetry—in distinctly latitudinarian ways. Yet I think it would be mistaken to say that Morton's idea of "Canaan" is simply a utopian (or, depending on one's point of view, dystopian) antithesis to Winthrop's sacred polis. Rather, Morton seems to be envisioning a form of settlement *larger* than Winthrop's at Boston—or Endicott's at Salem, or Bradford's at Plymouth—a settlement that would subsume all these others into itself, as a great metropolis gradually does its first suburbs. If one of the goals of colonial promotion is to make an alien place familiar, then Morton's goal is to make it familiar to those who not only live in London but prefer doing so, who would rather live there than anywhere else.

I stress this "urbanist" aspect of *New English Canaan* in contrast to the prevailing critical view of the book as an odd combination of pastoral celebration of the land and satirical critique of the land's Puritan inhabitants. The first and second books present relatively sober discussions of, respectively, the "manners & Customs" of the local Native Americans and "the beauty of the Country with her natural endowments." The second book does offer several passages that recall the heightened pastoral rhetoric of the Elizabethans, most notably Morton's description at the beginning of chapter 1 of his early impressions of the New England terrain:

> I did not think that in all the known world it could be paralleled, for so many goodly groves of trees, dainty fine round rising hillocks, delicate fair large plains; sweet crystal fountains and clear-running streams that twine in fine meanders through the meads, making so sweet a murmuring noise to hear as would even lull the senses with delight a sleep, so pleasantly do they glide upon the pebble stones, jetting most jocundly where they do meet and hand in hand run down to Neptunes Court, to pay the yearly tribute which they owe to him as sovereign Lord of all the springs.

He concludes, sliding into prosody, that "in my eye t'was Natures Masterpiece; Her chiefest Magazine of all where lives her store: if this Land be not rich, then is the whole world poor." For all Morton's application of Spenserian sensuousness to the prospect, the key word in the passage is "Magazine"—a warehouse where supplies (typically of a military character) are kept. The first of prefatory poems to the book, "In laudem Authoris," by the still unidentified gentleman "R. O.," speaks of "Fair Canaans second self, second to none, / Natures rich Magazine till now unknown," and invites the reader to "survey what nature hath in store." The metaphor of the magazine evidently bears repeating, as does the phrase "Natures Masterpiece," which appears in Morton's letter to the Privy Council at the front of the volume.[9] Nature's "store," then, is packed away in New Canaan's magazine, presumably waiting to be transported back to Europe by the ships that ply the passages of "Neptunes Court." The last clause of Morton's description offers not only a hyperbolic comparison but also a kind of admonition: if the "whole world" should choose not to acknowledge that "this Land" is "rich," then the whole world will be the poorer for lacking the treasures contained within "Natures Masterpiece."

Morton's vision of the new (as well as English) Canaan is founded on the mercantile, or at least material, model represented by the magazine. The precedent for this vision is readily available in the Old Testament's presentation of Canaan as the archetypal land of plenty; that is, Canaan as providing an abundance of the resources that allow for civilized existence. It is most certainly a consecrated place, and it certainly stands above the wicked cities of the plain, but it is also understood as the site of Jerusalem, a great city fed by the milk and honey of the hills. Morton's desire is to build upon the existing wealth of nature, as he indicates in his own prefatory poem, "The Authors Prologue": "If art and industry should do as much / As Nature hath for Canaan, not such / Another place, for benefit and rest, / In all the universe can be possest."[10] Whatever Morton means by "rest" in this passage, it is clearly not inertia, since "art and industry" are required to achieve it, and "Nature" by itself is not enough. Probably Morton means to indicate something like settlement—the idea of people coming to rest in a particular place where they will find "benefit."

The rest of the poem is taken up with the familiar trope of the uncolonized land as "a faire virgin, longing to be sped / And meet her lover in a Nuptial bed," a virgin who is "most fortunate / When most enjoyed." Presently Canaan's "fruitful womb" is a "glorious tomb" for lack of a proper English bridegroom—and almost surely Morton intends to suggest that Puritans make inadequate husbands in this sense, among others. He ends the poem by claiming, with a thoroughly awkward metaphorical turn, that his book will provide an "abstract" of the contents of the womb/tomb, showing the worth of those "Admired things" that now, redundantly, "lie fast bound in dark obscurity."[11] What he intends to expose to the light of day is not merely an inventory of things but the prospect of those things in a particular arrangement, for which Canaan provides— to borrow the words that Morton uses to praise his sometime patron Ferdinando Gorges—"the index or Lodestar." The arrangement, interestingly enough, is one where material riches are the seminal source of cultural riches.

Landskipp and Prospect:
Morton versus William Wood

Morton goes on to describe his "abstract" as a kind of pictorial essay at the end of chapter 1 of the first book:

> The riches of . . . [New England] I have set forth in this abstract as in a
> Landskipp, for the better information of the Travelers; which he may

peruse and plainly perceive by the demonstration of it, that it is nothing inferior to Canaan of Israel, but a kind of parallel to it in all points.[12]

Morton's choice of "Landskipp" as an analogue to his project is notable, since this term (according to the *OED* definition of *landscape,* a "corrupt" form of the word that predates the normative English form in print) was a relatively recent introduction at the time that Morton wrote his book, and it has a specific application to paintings of nonmarine scenery such as were produced in the Netherlands in great numbers during the seventeenth century. There is no way of knowing whether Dutch landscape painting influenced Morton's use of the term, but in the 1630s Holland was certainly the dominant outlet of such painting in northern Europe, and the Dutch style of landscape art circulated widely (it is also interesting to note that the first edition of *New English Canaan* was printed in Amsterdam).

In general, what distinguishes this style is the ubiquity of human activity and human artifacts in an otherwise rural prospect. In discussing the issue of "staffage," Wolfgang Stechow observes, "A Dutch painting of that period without any figures is a phenomenon of great rarity. . . . [E]ven in the most 'romantic' examples . . . complete lack of staffage is an exception." The significance of this, Stechow says, is

> that man does not lose himself in nature, that there is no attempt at a glorification or deification of nature as something beyond man's scope or control. A herdsman with cattle, a hunter of rabbits, a traveller on horseback talking to a man on foot . . . —these are the figures that animate the typical Dutch seventeenth-century landscape of the mature period.

In historical terms, the result of this "animation" and "human scale" was "a nature everybody was able to grasp and to recognize."[13] Moreover, many Dutch landscapes verge on the suburban: they depict roadways, canals, and fields on the outskirts of towns, with houses, farm buildings, church steeples, and windmills in the background and, frequently enough, the foreground as well. The work of Jan van Goyen in the 1620s and 1630s is typical in this regard. When Morton invokes the "Landskipp" at the beginning of *New English Canaan,* he is most likely thinking of it not as a picture of wilderness (or, for the more materially inclined, of an unorganized horn of plenty) but as a landscape both peopled and built.

Morton is also presenting his "Landskipp" as a counter to a "prospect"—specifically *New England's Prospect,* by William Wood, first published in 1634 and issued in a corrected edition a year later; this book was popular enough to reach a third edition in 1639, after *New English Canaan* had already fallen out of public view. There is obvious evidence in Morton's book that he views Wood as a competitor, since several times, mostly in the second book, he refers dismissively to a "wodden prospect" or "woodden prospect" that fails to serve the needs of knowledgeable observers.[14]

Wood's career is poorly documented, but he apparently spent several years in New England prior to 1633, when he returned to England. His book, according to the title page, purports to be "A true, lively, and experimental description . . . discovering the state of that Country, both as it stands to our new-come *English* Planters; and to the old Native Inhabitants. Laying down that which may both enrich the knowledge of the mind-traveling Reader, or benefit the future Voyager." Accordingly *New England's Prospect* is divided into two parts: the first is a discussion of the region as a site for English plantation, with chapters on topography, climate, soil, vegetation, animal life, and practical issues associated with colonial habitation; the second is an account of the customs and regional differences of the "Native Inhabitants"—as the heading to the second part indicates ("Of the Indians, Their Persons, Clothings, Diet, Natures, Customs, Laws, Marriages, Worships, Conjurations, Wars, Games, Huntings, Fishings, Sports, Language, Death, and Burials").[15]

The book is unusual for Wood's relative indifference to the conventions of promotional literature as he builds his argument on behalf of New England; he begins his preface, "To the Reader," by saying that he "will promise . . . no such voluptuous discourse as many have made upon a scanter subject." His consistent tactic throughout the book is not to make bold assertions about New England or the English colonial project but to correct, in a consistently temperate manner, various misguided assumptions about the conditions that potential settlers would confront upon reaching their destinations. Thus he devotes considerable space to demonstrating that the New England climate is in fact a healthy one (as opposed to *the* healthiest one). The second part presents the Native American population as an exotic but benign presence, one that cohabits easily with the English settlers:

> To enter into a serious discourse concerning the natural conditions of these Indians might procure admiration from the people of any civilized nations, in regard of their civility and good natures. If a tree may be judged by his fruit, and dispositions calculated by exterior actions, then may it be concluded that these Indians are of affable, courteous, and well-disposed natures, ready to communicate the best of their wealth to the mutual good of one another.[16]

The overall effect of the book is to convey an idea of the plantation of New England as a natural, self-evident process, one that hardly brooks debate or requires support. In this light, it is striking that Wood has nothing to say about the religious character of the early New England settlements; reading this book in the absence of any other information, one would be led to think that the colonization of New England was a secular enterprise.

New English Canaan presents conspicuous differences from *New England's Prospect,* differences that are quite likely intentional on Morton's part. He takes the unusual step of placing his discussion of the Native Americans first, whereas Wood (and, indeed, almost every colonial tract dating back to Harriot) places it last. Where Wood ignores the Puritans, Morton brings them constantly into view. Much of this seems motivated by Morton's awareness that the two books have inescapable generic affinities, since they emerge out of the same topos, so to speak. In order to distinguish his book in this "crowd," Morton is at pains to show that *his* landscape is better rendered than Wood's. Yet, self-interested as his remarks might be, Morton does have a point when he alludes to the "wooden prospect." Wood's prospect is, indeed, curiously wooden, in the sense that Wood shows little concern with the activities of the current *actual* planters in New England. Seelye has suggested that "Latent in Wood's [metaphorical] diagram is the idea of New England as a grand machine."[17] If Wood indeed does envision the landscape as a form of machinery, he has more difficulty depicting its human operators.

There are natural commodities, and there are communities of Native Americans, but Wood's interest in English settlers remains fairly abstract. He rarely mentions names, usually employing "the inhabitants" or an undifferentiated "they" to designate the colonists, and he offers little in the way of personal anecdote to season his discussion. Chapter 10 of the first part, "Of the Several Plantations in Particular," offers a series of portraits of towns that, for descriptive purposes, seem to contain very few people. Morton's own neighborhood of Mount Wollaston is described as "a very fertile soil, and a place very convenient for farmers' houses, there being great store of plain ground without trees." Whether Mount Wollaston actually has either houses or farmers is unclear in the passage. Wood's discussion of Boston is more detailed, dwelling at some length on the local scarcity of timber and pasturage, but even so the point of view is distant and impersonal:

> This town, although it be neither the greatest nor the richest, yet it is the most noted and frequented, being the center of the plantations where the monthly courts were kept. . . . Here likewise dwells the governor. This place hath very good land, affording rich cornfields and fruitful gardens, having likewise sweet and pleasant springs.[18]

The passive constructions in the first sentence serve to muffle any sense of the particularity of life in "the center of the plantations," and Wood lends no more attention to the presence there of the unnamed governor (Winthrop, of course) than he does to the peninsula's "very good land" and "sweet and pleasant springs."

Morton presents his "landskipp," then, as an alternative to the view in *New England's Prospect,* with its relative absence of human interest. In *New English Canaan* he is intent on presenting a picture of New England with plentiful and diverse "staffage" in the midst of forest and plain: Puritans, Native Americans, servants, adventurers, fur traders, passing acquaintances, and, in book 3, a range of vivid comic figures like Master Bubble, the Captains Littleworth and Shrimp, and the Barren Doe of Virginia. Taken together, these inhabitants of the landscape create the impression of a place already well settled and well traveled, not as far from the metropolis as its distance from London might indicate.

In other words, New England is a place already *in use,* in recognizably conventional ways; the question is whether it is being used in the proper ways. For Morton, more explicitly than for many early colonial writers, this question is framed not only in commercial but in cultural terms. The settlers that Morton sarcastically calls "Christians" have failed at efficiently exporting both the goods of and the facts about New England: they "have labored to keep both the practice of the people there, and the Real worth of that eminent Country concealed from public knowledge."[19] But they have also failed at importing what from Morton's point of view is the best commodity of old England—the metropolis itself, or at least the ambience of the metropolis. In a sense, Morton presents himself in *New English Canaan* as an agent in both import and export, importing a version of English urban culture that many of the inhabitants wish to reject, while exporting back to his putative audience in London the idea that such a culture can thrive in the marshes and stony woods around Massachusetts Bay. Whatever form Morton thinks this audience might take, and however large he thinks it might be, he evidently thinks it includes a contingent of *urbane* readers, which is to say readers who are comfortable with the contradictions of life in and around cities, where splendor and squalor, civility and rudeness, high art and scurrility are mingled in frequently inextricable ways. I will now turn to Morton's specific efforts to appeal to this putative group of readers.

Worthy Wights: Morton and Ben Jonson

At some point in his young adulthood, Morton received legal training at Clifford's Inn, one of the Inns of Chancery falling under the purview of the Inner Temple. His apparently formative experience among the Inns of Court has been a frequent point of reference for scholars of Morton, despite the paucity of documentary evidence about his activities and the duration of his stay there. Likewise, Morton's readers have frequently cited Ben Jonson as a significant influence on the style of *New English Canaan,* given Jonson's close personal connections with various members of the Inns from the late 1590s through at least the first decade of the seventeenth century.[20] There are certainly general affinities between Jonson's dramatic output and Morton's writing in the third book—the foundation of royalist conservatism under a seemingly irreverent surface; the fierce, even angry quality of the satire; the basic scorn of Puritanism and its practitioners (one thinks of Tribulation Wholesome in *The Alchemist* and Zeal-of-the-Land Busy in *Bartholomew Fair*); the use of poetic interludes and other devices associated with the art of the masque—but in fact there is only a single potential allusion to one of Jonson's plays in *New English Canaan:* at the end of the fifth chapter in book 2, Morton refers to "Lady Woodbees black gray-malkin," which would have "pastime enough" with the "good store" of mice in New England.[21] Lady Would-be is the insufferably talkative wife of Sir Politic Would-be in Jonson's *Volpone;* she also makes a cameo appearance in his short poem "To Fine Lady Would-Be" (*Epigrammes* 62), though at no point in the play (or the poem) does she appear to own a cat.[22]

A more obvious sign of Morton's debt to Jonson occurs at the beginning of the longest poem in *New English Canaan,* the "Baccanal Triumphe" that takes up most of chapter 17 in book 3. Opposite the first line is the marginal gloss "Master Ben: Jonson." The initial five lines of Morton's poem directly imitate the lines that introduce the second section of Jonson's "On the Famous Voyage," the last and longest poem in his collection *Epigrammes,* which appeared along with several other collections of Jonson's verse in the famous *Works* of 1616.

> I sing th' adventures of nine worthy wights,
> And pity 't is I cannot call them Knights,
> Since they had brawn and brain, and were right able
> To be installed of Prince Arthurs table;
> Yet all of them were Squires of low degree.
> ("Baccanal Triumphe," 1–5)

> I Sing the brave adventure of two wights,
> And pity 'tis, I cannot call 'hem knights:
> One was; and he for brawn, and brain, right able
> To have been styled of King ARTHURS table.
> The other was a squire, of fair degree.
> ("On the Famous Voyage," 21–25)[23]

That Jonson's name in the gloss carries the honorific "Master" suggests Morton's discipleship to a Jonsonian poetic sensibility; yet after these five mirrored lines, the literal narrative content of the "Bacchanal Triumph" parts ways with that of "On the Famous Voyage." Morton's poem, which he may have circulated among his acquaintances in London during his sojourn there in 1628–1629 (or so he seems to suggest), describes the plot of the "nine worthy wights" to suppress and capture the seven-headed Hydra, "which they misconster / Unto their land would prove a hideous monster" (9–10). As Morton explains in the following "Illustrations" to the poem, "it is to be considered that the Persons at Ma-re-Mount were seven, and they had seven heads and 14. feet; these were accounted Hydra with the seven heads: and the Maypole, with the Horns nailed near the top, was the forked tale of this supposed Monster."[24] Jonson's poem, on the other hand, recounts the upstream "voyage" of two gentlemen, Sheldon and Heydon, upon Fleet Ditch, the notorious river-turned-open-sewer that ran from Hampstead to the Thames, passing near the Inns of Court. (Fleet Ditch is also the locus for the final lines of Jonathan Swift's "A Description of a City Shower," a poem for which the lesser-known "On the Famous Voyage" is clearly a model.)

As a result, Morton's critics have paid little attention to the relation of Morton's poem to Jonson's; at least they have not done so in the middle register that falls between exposing outright textual homage and tracing more abstract forms of literary influence. Part of this neglect has to do with the fact that scholars of early-seventeenth-century English literature have tended to shy away from "On the Famous Voyage," one of the most aggressively scatological poems in the conventional canon. Adams in his note on the "Baccanal Triumphe" cannot even bring himself to mention the poem's title; he refers to it as "one of Jonson's productions, for a poem it is not." In an amusing display of prudery, Adams goes so far as to proclaim the "Bacchanal Triumph" preferable to Jonson's "productions" in general: "the verses in the *New Canaan* are, it must in justice be said, not only more cleanly, but in other respects superior to those to be found in Jonson's works. Indeed, where the latter are not unintelligible, they are almost unequalled for the nastiness in which the writer seems to revel." (Adams here seems to be thinking more of Jonson's plays than of his poetry.) Jonson's great modern editors C. H. Herford and Percy Simpson call it variously "a boisterous freak of stercoraceous humour," a "hideous and unsavoury burlesque," and "a bad joke which by way of a further joke, equally bad, . . . [Jonson] chose to include" in *Epigrammes.*[25]

Andrew McRae, in a recent (and rare) sustained interpretation of the poem, has used more judicious terms, describing "On the Famous Voyage" as a combination of "satire and saturnalia" that "maps a journey through a grotesque urban body."[26] As Sheldon and Heydon make their way by wherry up Fleet Ditch in search of a whorehouse that will accommodate them, Jonson presents scenes of ever more phantasmagorical squalor. The two men first encounter a "monster, / Ycleped *Mud,* which . . . / Belch'd forth an air, as hot, as at the muster / Of all your night-tubs, when the carts do cluster, / Who shall discharge first his merd-urinous load" (61–65). In a parody of the underworld journey of classical epic, they later encounter the "ghosts" of "farts, but late departed" (124–25) and the "*Fleet*-lane *Furies*" that along with "hot cooks . . . / . . . make the place *hell*" (143–44) with the by-products of cookery: "The sinks ran grease, and hair of measled hogs, / The heads, houghs, entrails, and the hides of dogs: / For, to say truth, what scullion is so nasty, / To put the skins, and offal in a pasty?" (145–48). Finally the spirit of "Old BANKS the juggler"— historically a London impresario who, in the poem, has for no obvious reason been transformed into a large cat—admonishes Sheldon and Heydon, asking them how their "dainty nostrils" could "Tempt such a passage? when each privys seat / Is fill'd with buttock? And the walls do sweat / Urine and plasters?" (165, 168–70). Banks then tells them that their journey is in vain, since the madam of the Holborn whorehouse "Is now from home" (181). The voyage concludes with the two men "Calling for RADAMANTHUS, that dwelt by, / A soap-boiler; and ÆACUS him nigh, / Who kept an ale-house; with my little MINOS, / An ancient purblind fletcher, with a high nose" (187–90), so that these three can "witness" to Sheldon and Heydon's "most liquid deed" (191, 193).[27]

Little of Jonson's imagery or specific conception survives in Morton's "Baccanal Triumph." Other than the five lines of imitation at the outset, the poem's main borrowing consists of "Minos, Eacus, and Radamand, / Princes of Limbo" (49–50). In Greek mythology, Radamanthus, Æecus, and Minos were the three judges of the dead in Hades, male counterparts to the Fates. Tellingly in these lines, Morton substitutes a Christian (though not Protestant) variant of the underworld for a pagan one; in the none-too-hidden allegory of the poem, Morton/Hydra is very much in "Limbo," both because from the perspective of his enemies he is effectually

one of the unbaptized, and because he is caught on the threshold between one state and another—not quite eligible for eternal damnation,
but not an assimilable colonist either. Whomever Morton intends as the
members of his judicial trio (Adams favors Standish for Minos, Samuel
Fuller for Eacus, and Bradford for Radamand), their activity is clear enough:
they decide that Hydra ought to be hauled in irons before the gods, "To
be accused on the upper ground / Of Lese Majestatis, this crime found /
T'will be unpossible from thence, I trow / Hydra shall come to trouble us
below" (71–74). Having agreed on a course of action, they celebrate in decidedly nonsectarian fashion:

> The Sessions ended, some did straight devise
> Court revels, antics and a world of joys,
> Brave Christmas gambols: there was open hall
> Kept to the full, and sport, the Devil and all:
> Labor's despised, the looms are laid away,
> And this proclaim'd the Stygian Holiday.
> In came grim Mino, with his motley beard,
> And brought a distillation well prepared;
> And Eacus, who is as sure as text,
> Came in with his preparatives the next;
> Then Radamanthus, last and principal,
> Feasted the Worthies in his sumptuous hall.
> There Charon Cerberus and the rout of fiends
> Had lap enough: and so their pastime ends. (78–91)[28]

Given that this concluding scene takes place in the underworld, it can
be understood as the parody of a "proper" celebration; it is, nonetheless,
a celebration, specifically in the style of "Court revels." (Whether this
phrase refers to the royal court or the Inns of Court will have to remain
an open question, since "revels" did occur in both venues.) These revels
are also not far removed from the ones that Morton and his cohort had
performed around the maypole, as described in chapter 14 of *New English
Canaan*.[29] What is distinctive in the passage, and the poem as a whole, is
that Morton maintains his jocular, ironic detachment, neither moralizing
nor lapsing into invective in regard to his opponents at Plymouth—both
of which rhetorical gestures he is certainly prone to in other parts of the
third book. There is a certain *glee* on Morton's part in imagining the likes

of Bradford and Standish engaging in festive behavior similar to what he himself has commemorated in chapter 14. Their "pastime" simply "ends," without Morton passing further judgment on the participants.

It is true that Morton assumes this more tolerant stance within the confines of a poem, formally distinct from the prose that surrounds it. As a writer of prose, on the other hand, Morton accuses the Bay separatists of multiple crimes ranging from felonies to peccadilloes: of treacherously murdering Native Americans at Wessagusset (thus, he claims, causing the local tribes "from that time afterwards" to "call the English Planters Wotawquenange, which in their language signifieth stabbers, or Cutthroats");[30] of derogating the Book of Common Prayer as an "idol: and those that use it, Idolaters," and of imposing cruel and unusual punishments on nonprofessors;[31] of mounting Machiavellian campaigns of public defamation against their opponents; and of closing their eyes at prayer, "because they think themselves so perfect in the high way to heaven that they can find it blindfold: so do not I."[32]

By translating Morton's characterization of the separatists into the realm of mock epic and comic allegory, the "Baccanal Triumphe" offers a respite of sorts from the pugnacious, often sour satire that prevails in the third book. Morton the poet takes a more Olympian view of the matter; he is a man of culture viewing the folly of the world from an aestheticized distance. The three judges still belong to that world, even if they occupy the lowest part of it. Morton complains at various times in the third book about "the payment you shall get, if you be one of them they term, without,"[33] yet this poem suggests that Morton is not entirely invested in paying the separatists back in kind. In Morton's verse, at least, even his staunchest enemies are not "without."

This last point brings me back to the nature of Morton's debt to Jonson, which has more to do with authorial voice and point of view than with the use of specific poetic devices. Jonson refrains from judging Sheldon and Heydon's bizarre journey in any explicitly moral way. The content of "On the Famous Voyage" could easily provide him with fuel for a fierce critique of the physical and moral deficiencies of urban life, but—as is also usually the case with similar content in his city comedies— it primarily seems to fuel Jonson's productivity as an artist. McRae observes that the material of the poem "looks towards filth and corruption but evokes simultaneously a strangely subversive vitality," and the anarchic world that Jonson describes "also fosters a distinctive creativity, evident as much in the tumultuous character of Jonson's distended epigram as it is in the grotesque environment of the London underworld."[34] By virtue of its allusiveness, its deep awareness of classical precedent and traditional idioms, and its rhetorical ingenuity—by the very fact of its existence—the poem suggests that higher orders of expression, perhaps even of being, can be generated out of the detritus of contemporary experience. Obnoxious as its surfaces and textures might be, "On the Famous Voyage" also has a metonymic relation with the stuff of high literary culture, available in many other forms in the *Epigrammes* and in more conventional poems of place such as "To Penshurst." In this reading, London becomes (to borrow from Mary Shelley's *Frankenstein*) the "filthy workshop of creation" from which a greater work—rather than a monster—finally emerges.

What Morton inherits from Jonson, then, is the idea that poems can generate a sensibility apart from their nominal content—can generate, in other words, a broader, "cosmic" understanding of persons, things, and events, one that emerges from but does not finally depend on the particulars described in the poems themselves. Poetry is certainly common enough in colonial texts, but Morton's effort to present his poems as centrally significant to the narrative of the third book suggests that he attributes considerable heuristic power to them, however cryptic they may seem to present-day readers. Morton carefully introduces each of the poems in the third book as being intrinsic to the history of his stay in New England, rather than being only retrospective commentary on that history. "Time, that brings all things to light" is an epitaph commemorating the death of the Barren Doe's infant son; the "Carmen Elegiacum" originates out of the Barren Doe's plea that a gentleman write a letter of complaint on her behalf to her absconded lover; "Rise Oedipus" is nailed to the maypole as official notice (to the Pilgrims, apparently) that Morton has named the place Ma-re Mount; "Drink and be merry, merry, merry boys" is sung by a "Chorus" around the maypole; "What ails Pygmalion?" purports to describe the new coat of arms of an anonymous "tomb maker" whom Master Temperwell (Winthrop) has promoted over a more worthy settler; and both the "Baccanal Triumphe" and Christopher Gardiner's sonnet are presented as personal responses to specific instances of persecution by the separatists.[35]

To revert to the metaphor of the "landskipp," the poetry allows for a longer perspective, a more remote vanishing point, a more complex rendering of the "space" of New England. There may be a fair amount of condescension in this, as there often is in Jonson's poetic stance; one is aware of the author/artist operating above the scene, apart from the action. But for Morton, this aspect of poetic discourse provides a valuable counterbalance to what is otherwise a bitter if farcical screed concerning his victimization by men whom he wishes to regard as his moral and intellectual inferiors. The reasoning would appear to be that to situate one's enemies inside a poem is an effective way of shrinking their dimensions and reestablishing a proper sense of proportion.

In Chapter 1, I talked about the phenomenon of competing rationales in the *Generall Historie of Virginia,* mainly in terms of the ways that John Smith conceptualized his experiences at Jamestown. In *New English Canaan,* these competing rationales are indicated formally. The *prosaic* thesis of the third book is, simply put, that the separatists ought to be removed from power in New England, to be replaced by those who, like Morton, better represent "authentic" English values. As Michael Zuckerman has pointed out,

> It was Morton . . . who bore the culture of the mother country most nearly in colonial New England. It was he who tried to maintain the rituals of the English heritage, he who preached the latitudinarian notions of the English church, he who preserved the bawdy, ebullient spirit of the Elizabethans.

For all the carrying-on at Ma-re Mount, Morton (like Jonson) is in many ways a staunch social conservative, and this strain in his character has led Cartelli to argue that *New English Canaan* shares "the same polemically-charged discourse of contempt and exclusion" that emerges from separatist texts.[36]

Morton's *poetic* thesis, however, is more complex. Here the separatists belong among the subjects of the "landskipp," as it were; they might be aggravating, they might even at times be dangerous, but they are still intrinsic to the picture, if merely as the butts of Morton's jokes. They provide a necessary degree of friction for generating energy in the great "magazine" of this second Canaan; they contribute signally to the tussle of interests that mark New England as a productive place—productive not only of nature's goods but of the cultural goods that result from "art and industry." In an intriguing presentation of Morton's activities as a radical effort to transform the way information circulated in early New England, Matt Cohen argues that *"New English Canaan* makes a sophisticated argument for a plural, literate culture of intellectual exchange," based on Morton's experience of such exchange in London: "In Morton's world, masques performed at the Inns of Court and royal proclamations had equal status as legitimate public communications. Both were part of a spectrum of intellectual and political activity that could not be considered centralized."[37]

If Morton could cultivate such a decentralized mode of exchange, one where his words would matter as much as those of Bradford, Winthrop, or Endicott, then the Bay region, despite its lack of a single imposing town, *could* be like London, generating a rich local discourse out of its disparate and often disordered parts. The main caveat is that there are not yet enough other colonists of the "right" sort—that is, like Morton—in New England to allow the separatists to be absorbed properly into the cultural mélange. Accordingly, Morton appeals to a cosmopolitan readership (if perhaps one that only exists in his imagination) to join him in the enterprise of transforming the community that constantly seeks to exclude him and others like him. In its own peculiar way, *New English Canaan* is a plea for immigration as a tool for creating a more diverse population—for adding more gentiles, so to speak, to balance the scales with the self-designated "Israelites" of Massachusetts.

Mine Host in Nineveh

The "landskipp" that Morton portrays in his book presents an alternative nexus for communal life in New England: the public house or tavern, rather than the congregational meetinghouse. Where the meetinghouse serves to shelter a commonly held set of beliefs, a unified sense of purpose, and a faith in the stability and permanence of the institutions that have motivated people to gather there, the public house celebrates the power of commerce to bind and loose in largely secular ways. By design it honors transience, providing a fixed point for people who are merely passing through from one place to another, a site not only for eating, drinking, and sleeping but for buying, selling, and otherwise transacting business. Its lingua franca is the exchange value of goods and services, and its promise of hospitality is inextricably linked to the dynamics of trade.

Morton, of course, refers to himself throughout *New English Canaan* as "Mine Host," the welcoming proprietor of such an establishment. Interestingly, he accuses the "beggars" of England—the various unemployed and masterless men who were a constant source of concern to the English authorities during the sixteenth and seventeenth centuries—of being unwilling to abandon their Old World taverns to make the voyage to a better life in New England:

> But they of this sort of our own nation, that are fit to go to this Canaan . . . [are] most of them unwilling to go from the good ale tap, which is the very lodestone of the land by which our English beggars steer their Course; it is the Northpole to which the flower-de-luce of their compass points.[38]

Morton, as it were, wishes to substitute the maypole of Ma-re Mount for the "Northpole" of the "good ale tap" back in England. In any case, his primitive trading post at the wood's edge would hardly be mistaken for a London public house, but his foes evidently saw the affinity and did what they could to force it out of operation (even so, public houses quickly emerged in and around Boston in the seventeenth century to play their customary role in community life).[39] I am less concerned here, obviously, with the practical value of Ma-re Mount as the source of Morton's livelihood than in its symbolic value in *New English Canaan*'s presentation of the Bay region as hospitable for colonists other than Pilgrims and Puritans. What Standish and Endicott managed to destroy, Morton rebuilds in the pages of his book, especially in the third section. As he describes the campaign against Ma-re Mount and against his projects in general, he also conveys a sense of the kind of discourse that emanates from the public house (as opposed to the meetinghouse): freewheeling, witty, erudite, ironic, urbane, and biased toward the comic rather than the tragic in human experience.

Whether or not Ma-re Mount still physically stands, the idea that it *once* stood and that revels were held there is sufficient reassurance that there might be place and profit for the sophisticated denizens of the Inns of Court even in a land overrun with separatists. The praise of "Nectar" in the song sung around the maypole in chapter 14 metaphorically suggests the salutary value of Morton's "public" discourse:

> Nectar is a thing assign'd
> By the Deities own mind
> To cure the heart oppressed with grief,
> And of good liquors is the chief.
> . . . .
> Give to the Melancholy man
> A cup or two of 't now and then;
> This physic will soon revive his blood,
> And make him be of a merrier mood. (11–14, 17–20)[40]

Perhaps it goes without saying that for this nectar to have its proper effect on the various melancholy men in Massachusetts Bay Colony, there would have to more places like Ma-re Mount, not fewer. In promoting his vision of an artistic and intellectual as well as appetitive "street life" that thrives in spite of the antipathy of a significant part of the local population, Morton is probably the earliest writer associated with New England to purvey an *aesthetic* account of the colonial scene that is not essentially pastoral.

He also represents himself as a prophet without honor in his adopted country, but rather than assuming the role of an Isaiah or a Jeremiah, he borrows, interestingly enough, the mantle of Jonah. In the last chapter of *New English Canaan,* he recounts his forced return to England in 1630–1631 aboard a "pitiful weather beaten ship, where mine Host was in more danger, (without all question,) then Jonas, when he was in the Whales belly." Having safely gotten ashore in England, he "began in a posture like Jonas, and cried, Repent you cruel Schismatics, repent; there are as yet but 40. days, if Jove vouchsafe to thunder, Charter and the Kingdom of the Separatists will fall asunder: Repent you cruel Schismatics, repent." The allegorical connections are less than precise here, for in the book of Jonah in the Old Testament, Jonah delivered his message—

"Yet forty days, and Nineveh shall be overthrown" (Jonah 3:4)—from *within* the city of Nineveh. At this point Morton was, strictly speaking, more than a thousand miles from the "city" where he meant to be heard; he conveyed his words "by letters returned into new Canaan," but the Old Testament offers no precedent for epistolary prophets.[41] In any event, Morton's Ninevites would undoubtedly argue that they had long since "turned from their evil way" (Jonah 3:10) and could safely ignore a prophet of doom from "without."

There is ample evidence here, as elsewhere in *New English Canaan*, that Morton does not mean to be taken completely seriously. Yet in light of the aspects of the book that I have been exploring here, it is worth considering the elements of Jonah's narrative that Morton leaves unstated. In the book of Jonah—perhaps the closest thing to a shaggy dog story in the entire Bible—the reluctant prophet is enraged when God, seeing the swift repentance of the Ninevites, chooses not to destroy them. "So Jonah went out of the city, and sat on the east side of the city, and there made him a booth, and sat under it in the shadow, till he might see what would become of the city" (Jonah 4:5). In effect, God playfully teases Jonah, first causing a gourd to grow over his head to shade him, then sending a worm to make the gourd wither, then tormenting him with "a vehement east wind" and hot sun (4:8). All of this makes Jonah still more irate: "I do well to be angry, even unto death" (4:9). The tale concludes with God gently admonishing Jonah for his obstinacy:

> Thou hast pity on the gourd, for the which thou hast not laboured, neither madest it grow; which came up in a night, and perished in a night:
> And should not I spare Nineveh, that great city, wherein are more than sixscore thousand persons that cannot discern between their right hand and their left hand; and also much cattle? (4:10–11)

Perhaps, in the spirit of Jonah's story, Morton's anger at his maltreatment in Massachusetts will not prevail over the broader (even comic) theme, one that is implicit in the final pages of *New English Canaan*: God will spare Nineveh, "that great city," because its sum (that is, the sum of its goods) is greater than its (human) parts. Even if no city of this sort exists yet in New England, the value of the place is such that even cruel schismatics and other "persons that cannot discern between their left hand and their right hand" might be spared in pursuit of the greater prospects afforded by the proper exercise of "art and industry." Ultimately the "landskipp" of Morton's New Canaan is one in which his separatist enemies have a place within the frame—as caricatured figures in the middle distance of a prosperous market street—while in the foreground a grinning, rather supercilious-looking gentleman leans against the door of a tavern, writing something, maybe verse, in a notebook.

4

—⁓—

American Consciences

Roger Williams's Field of Inquiry

At *Providence* . . . lives master *Williams,* and his company of diverse opinions. . . . [T]hey hold there is no true visible Church in the *Bay,* nor in the world, nor any true Ministry.

—THOMAS LECHFORD, *Plain Dealing;*
or News from New-England (1642)

For we know in part, and we prophesy in part.
But when that which is perfect is come, then that which is in part shall be done away.

—1 CORINTHIANS 13:9–10

'Tis true, there is an edge in all firm belief, and with an easy Metaphor we may say the sword of faith; but in these obscurities I rather use it in the adjunct the Apostle gives it, a Buckler; under which I perceive a wary combatant may lie invulnerable.

—THOMAS BROWNE, *Religio Medici*

As a representative of dissent in the early colonial period, Roger Williams is considerably more famous—and more intellectually distinguished—than Thomas Morton; yet in terms of his place in the epistemological history of New England, Williams has remained almost as blurry a figure. My purpose in this chapter is to survey both the physical and metaphysical terrain on which Williams built his distinctive knowledge project, and thus to locate with greater precision his place in early colonial discourse. What I want to illuminate is the distinctive, even anomalous, open-endedness of Williams's writing during the 1640s on a variety of topics. In the previous chapters, I have frequently pointed out instances where colonial writing avoids or defies closure; what marks Williams as unusual is that the lack of closure comes across as *systematic* in an intellectual sense. There are good reasons, I would argue, for setting Williams apart from his book-writing coevals in New England, reasons that do not turn solely on his extreme (and stubbornly held) ecclesiological views.

My survey will turn on a comparison of Williams's two most important works, *A Key into the Language of America* and *The Bloudy Tenent of Persecution,* which appear close to each other in Williams's career (*Key into the Language* in 1643, *The Bloudy Tenent* in 1644) but which have rarely been discussed in tandem.[1] In fact, scholarship on Williams has generally followed one of two routes that are often in sight of each other but rarely seem to run over common ground. The first is, metaphorically speaking, the broad highway—we might call it the Vernon L. Parrington Memorial Turnpike and the Perry Miller Extension. Here Williams is a figure in the intellectual and political history of Puritanism both in Old and New England, a dissenter from seventeenth-century orthodoxy and a prophet of eighteenth-century liberalism (if not the father of religious toleration and the separation of church and state). The second path of Williams scholarship is more like a hunting track threading through the woods, though lately it has gotten wider, thanks to pioneers like Francis Jennings, Karen Ordahl Kupperman, Neal Salisbury, and Alden Vaughan. Here Williams is a prominent actor in the encounter between European and Native American in the early colonial period and is an important contributor to the ethnohistory of North America after 1607 (if not also a collaborator in the expansion of English settlement, and thus in the destruction of the New England tribes).

Williams's fellow travelers on the first route are the apostles of, and dissenters from, the New England Way—John Cotton, John Winthrop, Thomas Hooker, Anne Hutchinson; on the second, he is accompanied by a considerably less-exalted crew: Thomas Harriot, John Smith, Thomas Morton, William Wood, John Josselyn. On the first route he carries a copy of *The Bloudy Tenent,* the major installment in his lengthy debate with the great Anglo-American divine Cotton over the right of civil magistrates to

persecute religious heterodoxy, presented (rather loosely and very undra-
matically) as a long dialogue between Truth and Peace. On the second route,
he carries *Key into the Language,* the first of his surviving published works and
the first sustained attempt by an English speaker at a dictionary of a Native
American language, based on his experience among the Narragansetts after
his banishment from the Bay Colony in 1635 and containing a substantial
amount of valuable commentary on Native American lifeways as well as the
only surviving examples of Williams's efforts as a poet.

My reading of these two books leads me to say that the destination of
both routes is the same, that the same pilgrim is to be found on both, and
that whatever their local differences, the routes run through the same territory. In illustrating this claim, I will work backward to a degree, address-
ing *The Bloudy Tenent* in some detail before moving on to *Key into the
Language,* since the chronologically later work offers an explicit intellectual
context that remains elliptical in the earlier one. This procedure seems
justified given that both works are products (or at least by-products) of
Williams's journey to England in 1643–1644 in pursuit of a charter for the
Providence plantations. In any event, there is a notable consistency to his
thought from book to book; his writing may at times be difficult to follow
but his working principles are not, and they change little in either the
short or long term. Whether he presents himself as a theological controversialist or a nascent linguist, his purposes are to align his activity with
God's scripturally revealed plan for the human community, to remove the
obstacles to the unfolding of the divine will in history, and to help open
the way for Christ's triumphant return at the end of the age—which, in
Williams's view, can occur only after the New Testament, and the true
form of the church present within it, is embraced throughout the world.
John Garrett has briefly described this position:

> To Williams . . . the duty of the true Christian was to go out into the
> wilderness of a world wider than the settled congregation . . . [and] to
> wait for the fulfilment of the expectation that when the task of witness-
> ing was complete all would be set to rights, in both church and world,
> by Christ.[2]

Yet the first chapter of Garrett's biography is entitled "The Elusive
Roger Williams." Some of this elusiveness has to do with a scarcity of

straightforward biographical evidence, as Patricia Rubertone has pointed out:

> Simple facts such as the dates of his birth and death are not known with any certainty. Except for a thumbprint impressed into sealing wax, his physical attributes are a mystery. Even those who actually knew him, either as friends or adversaries, remembered less about him than other notable English colonists in the seventeenth century. Like the romantic images of him produced by later artists, he exists in the mind's eye as formal, distant, and benign. At best, he is vaguely familiar; at worst, generally indistinct.[3]

What initially seems simple enough to grasp—that Williams is a strict Calvinist with millenarian expectations and a strongly evangelical bent— has not led to any sort of lasting critical consensus about his life and work; he is as much an "American Sphinx" as that other legendary and oft-misappropriated sponsor of the American way, Thomas Jefferson.[4] This elusiveness has to do with the historical complexity of Williams's relationships with the world around him, and it also has to do with the character of his writing. Williams is an unusual (though certainly not unique) figure in that he moved in such radically different spheres during his career. One can imagine him grappling with doctrine in a Salem pulpit, writing by lamplight in London, arguing with Cotton, conversing with John Milton; one can envision him trading in furs, woolens, and pewter at Cocumscussoc, or sharing a meal, a fire, and a Bible lesson with a Narragansett chieftain at the edge of the forest, but it is hard to combine these into a single image of an urbane cleric who is also a missionary frontiersman. Williams's writing only compounds the problem: it often gives the impression of being the product of contingent circumstances, full of the energy and improvisation that circumstances generate but lacking the quality of meticulousness that suggests well-ordered activity.

This has resulted in quite a number of partial accounts of his accomplishments—"partial" in both senses, since scholars have seized on the aspects of his career that they find most accessible, usually based on their preferences for either the broad highway or the hunting track. For example, Miller, who in the fifties almost single-handedly revived interest in Williams as a theologian (though at some considerable cost to Williams's reputation as a thinker) described *Key into the Language* as a book with "no formal continuity. . . . [I]t consists merely of a list of words and phrases punctuated by seemingly random observations." This, Miller argued, "has prevented it from being studied by any but anthropologists." On the other hand, Myra Jehlen, in her contribution to the decidedly revisionist first volume of the Cambridge History of American Literature (1994), characterized *Key into the Language* as "Williams's most extensive and developed work" while completely ignoring *The Bloudy Tenent,* regarded by Miller as well as many other scholars as Williams's "masterpiece, the book which gives him his reputation with posterity."[5]

It should be possible to talk about these aspects of Williams, and the works that represent them, in the same chapter if not exactly in the same breath. I propose that one way to do this is according to the terms that I have gradually been outlining in this book: perhaps more than any of the other figures I am considering here, Williams illustrates in his writings the problem of reconciling a new world to a known world. It would be more accurate to say "new worlds," since there are at least two important ones for Williams, corresponding to the two routes that I have outlined above. The first "new world" is that of the evolving Puritan polities in both old and New England, and the second is that of the wilderness, the Indian territory at the boundary of English settlement. The known world, interestingly enough, is one that many present-day readers would consider more speculative than actual—the world of holy Scripture, of God's revealed word. For Williams, this is the stable ground of truth—familiar, inarguable, and, as he suggests in his 1644 pamphlet *Mr. Cottons Letter Examined and Answered,* the standard for all rational human judgments: "The Scriptures or *writings* of *truth* are those heavenly righteous *scales,* wherein all our controversies must be tried, and that blessed Star that leads all those *souls* to Jesus that seek him."[6]

In this understanding, of course, Williams is by no means alone. What makes his use of this known world compelling is that he so often places its certainty against, and in contest with, worlds that are manifestly uncertain—worlds that also happen to be the ones he lives in day to day. Such mental arrangements distinguish him from most other theologically oriented writers in New England, who, in pursuing the great questions of existence and eternity, were mainly content not to worry about how those outside their immediate community—specifically, Native Americans—might fit within the divine order. Williams, however, did worry about this question and the priority it ought to have within a true Christian practice.[7]

In Williams's case, this concern led to a form of experimental inquiry into how and to what purpose an absolute knowledge (which we would now be more likely to characterize as "faith" or "conviction") can be brought to bear in areas where one only sees, in Saint Paul's familiar words, "through a glass darkly." One of Williams's favorite epithets for God is "father of lights," which he invariably means in a more than celestial sense.[8] God, through the medium of Scripture, shines the light of reason into the mind of each believer: "tis Light alone," Williams declares in *The Bloudy Tenent,* "even Light from the bright shining Sun of Righteousness, which is able, in the souls and consciences of men to dispel and scatter such fogs and darkness." The "fogs and darkness" are properties of the world as it now stands; the figure of Peace puts the question rhetorically to the figure of Truth near the beginning of their dialogue: "What is the *Earth* but a *dungeon of darkness,* where *Truth* is not?" Light, Williams hopes, will guide the believer (and the reader) toward Truth—or, perhaps more accurately, toward a better sense of the obstacles that occlude a vision of Truth. For there are indeed many obstacles, vividly laid out in *The Examiner Defended,* one of the flurry of pamphlets that Williams produced in 1652: "Oh how many are the *Screens,* the *Veils,* the *Hoods,* the *Vizards,* the *Curtains,* the *Hangings,* the *Cloaks,* the *Clouds,* and *Colors,* by which the *luster* and *shining* of that which we call *Truth,* is hidden and eclipsed from us!" What does Williams mean here by "that which we call *Truth*"? To him, Scripture is in itself not particularly mysterious; his comments on biblical passages nearly always reflect his firm confidence in the rightness of his exegeses. The truth that remains so hidden from view appears rather to center on the relationship between the New Testament (for Williams, the only testament that really matters) and human history—between the revealed Word and an unrevealed world, so to speak. The object of rational inquiry is to identify the precise character of that relationship using what we could call the "available light": "beyond the light and persuasion of *conscience* can no man living walk in any fear of God."[9]

It is the pursuit of this inquiry, and not the inquiry into scriptural truth per se, that remains fraught with intellectual peril, for, as Peace asks in *The Bloudy Tenent,* "how strong *delusions* are, and *believing* of *lies,* and how hard it is to be undeceived, especially in *Spirituals?*" Truth has observed just previously in the text that even committed believers are easily deceived: "Yea Gods people themselves, being deluded and captivated are strongly confident even against some fundamentals, especially of worship, and yet not against the light, but according to the light or eye of a deceived conscience." A proper approach to inquiry requires deep humility and an openness to more than one avenue through the screens, veils, hoods, and so on, that stand in the way of a correct knowledge of how humanity enacts, and ought to enact, the divine will. Williams's recognition of the long (indeed, continuing) history of human error in making sense of that will is what leads directly to his advocacy of religious toleration:

> [N]otwithstanding their confidence of the *truth* of their own way, yet the experience of our *Fathers errors,* our own *mistakes* and *ignorance,* the sense of our own *weaknesses* and *blindness* in the depths of the *prophesies* & *mysteries* of the Kingdom of *Christ,* and the great professed *expectation* of *light* to come which we are not now able to comprehend, may abate the edge, yea sheath up the *sword* of persecution toward any.[10]

The seventeenth century is one of the greatest periods for inquiries based on the *"expectation* of *light* to come which we are not now able to comprehend" (Thomas Browne's *Religio Medici*—published the same year as *Key into the Language*—and Blaise Pascal's *Pensées* come readily to mind), but Williams's work is exceptional in being written from such an explicitly colonial perspective. Possibly something of the same effect can be felt in Alvar Nuñez Cabeza de Vaca's *Naufragios* or Mary Rowlandson's *The Sovereignty and Goodness of God*—that is, an apparent loosening of the tether that ties the writer to the "rock" of his or her foundational beliefs— but this activity does not occur in either case with the deliberation that Williams brings to it.

Then again, neither Cabeza de Vaca nor Rowlandson understand their witness to the world in the way that Williams does. His primary concern is not to record his own experience, knowledge, or opinions, but to seek the ultimate ground of authenticity in human affairs. Like many Calvinists before (and after) him, Williams is painfully aware of the discrepancy between the foundational premises of the Gospels and the ability of believers to act upon them. The civil world—the world of magistracy, of laws and the institutions that enforce them—is itself a mark of the divorce between Christly and worldly patterns, since an authentic community of sanctified believers (a community that Williams has yet to find in New England) would be self-regulating (it would not require a magistracy to maintain itself in stability and health). Such a community, Williams argues in *The Bloudy Tenent*, is based on the soundest of historical models:

> the Scriptures of *Truth* and the *Records* of Time concur in this, that the first *Churches* of *Christ Jesus*, the *lights, patterns* and *precedents* to all succeeding Ages, were gathered and governed without the aid, assistance, or countenance of any Civil Authority, from which they suffered great persecutions for the name of the *Lord Jesus* professed amongst them.

To rediscover and restore these *"lights, patterns* and *precedents,"* one must step away from the unquestioned—or, worse, enforced—truisms of the civil world, to become a "separatist" at multiple levels. Thus, Williams's exile into what he calls on multiple occasions the "howling wilderness" of Narragansett Bay is indeed the model of (and for) Providence: it allows him to see his way through a primitive world toward the primitive truth.[11]

In *The Bloudy Tenent*, Williams describes truth's venues with figures that are both utterly familiar and suggestive of the colonial scene: "Precious *Pearls* and *Jewels*, and far more precious *Truth* are found in muddy shells and places. The rich *Mines* of *golden Truth* lie hid under barren hills, and in *obscure* holes and *corners*." The metaphors are homely, but they also gesture toward the putative resources of the American wilderness. Williams has already employed the same imagery in *Key into the Language*, in chapter 24 on Native American "coin"; after a detailed account of the varieties and enumerations of wampum (another treasure drawn from "muddy shells"), Williams offers the "general" observation that "The sons of men having lost their Maker, the true and only Treasure, dig down to the bowels of the earth for gold and silver; yea, to the bottom of the Sea, for shells of fishes, to make up a Treasure, which can never truly enrich or satisfy." This is followed (in the normal pattern of *Key into the Language*) by a "More particular" poem:

> The *Indians* prize not *English* gold,
> Nor *English Indians* shell:
> Each in his place will pass for ought,
> What ere men buy or sell.
>
> *English* and *Indians* all pass hence,
> To an eternal place,
> Where shells nor finest gold's worth ought,
> Where nought's worth ought but Grace.
>
> This coin the *Indians* know not of,
> Who knows how soon they may?
> The *English* knowing, prize it not,
> But fling't like dross away.[12]

As with many of Williams's poems in *Key into the Language,* this celebration of grace is none too graceful, but it remains thematically suggestive. Its argument is that value is relative to context; a currency has worth insofar as the people who use it find it worthwhile for their purposes. Grace is a divine currency, one not to be found in the marketplace since (following traditional Calvinist theology) it is only God's to give and to give freely—thus, paradoxically, a coin for which and in which there is no commerce. Obviously, neither English nor Indians have reached the "eternal place" where they will understand the actual worth of God's "coin," but the third stanza suggests that the Indians are in a place where there is at least the possibility that they will learn to value grace properly—a possibility that the English have perversely foreclosed to themselves. The poem builds its semantic tension on the antithesis of *ought* and *nought/not*, which grades finally into the assonance between *know* and *nought/not*. Between the poles of knowing and not knowing (or knowing nought), there is a third, speculative position signaled by the question "Who knows . . . ?" Williams's poem infers a vantage point from which such a question can be asked but not necessarily answered, a position slightly different from that of the Indians, who do not yet know how to ask the right questions, and entirely different from that of the English, who choose not to ask them at all—

perhaps because the answers, should they be forthcoming, would not be deemed acceptable.

Garden and Wilderness: The Place of the Witness in *The Bloudy Tenent of Persecution*

Should this vantage point simply be identified with Williams's own? Such has been the tendency among recent commentators on Williams—to treat him as an idiosyncratic observer with an extremely heightened, if not exaggerated, sense of his own singularity and significance upon the colonial scene.[13] But Williams, while he may rue the fact that there are few like-minded seekers, does not present (nor, I would say, does he conceive) himself to be the only person in New England who will ever ask such questions. The vantage point he offers has a more generic, even symbolic character: it is that of a witness in the wilderness.[14] Of the numerous well-known biblical exemplars of this figure, perhaps the most relevant would be the one to whom Cotton once compared Williams (to Williams's disadvantage): John of Patmos, the author of Revelation, exiled by the Roman emperor Domitian to a rugged and lonely island, where he recorded his vision of Christ's Second Coming and the restoration of Jerusalem—albeit, Cotton claimed, with far less self-pity than Williams displayed in writing from his place of exile.[15]

In the broad scheme of *The Bloudy Tenent,* such a witness would stand—whether voluntarily or under compulsion—outside of the civil world, a world transformed into Babel as a result of the magistracy's persecution of conscience. Truth argues that to be a citizen of Babel is, in effect, to babble, to think and speak confusedly:

> Oh it is hard for *Gods children* to fall to *opinion* and *practice* of *Persecution,* without the ready learning the *language* thereof: And doubtless, that Soul that can so readily speak *Babels* language, hath cause to fear that he hath not yet in point of Worship left the Gates or Suburbs of it.

From his position outside of the gates and beyond the suburbs, the witness recognizes that the wall between Babel and the wilderness is a false one, and (according to Truth) this has been the case at least since the time that Constantine instituted the civil punishment of heresy: *"Babel* or con-

fusion was usher'd in, and by degrees the *Gardens* of the *Churches* of *Saints* were turned into the *Wilderness* of whole *Nations,* until the *whole World* became *Christian* or *Christendom."* In this view, *"Christendom"* reflects a state of false consciousness; it is merely another name for the papacy, thus Antichrist's favorite euphemism. As Williams earlier observed in his discussion "Of *Beasts, &c."* in *Key into the Language,* "The Wilderness is a clear resemblance of the world, where greedy and furious men persecute and devour the harmless and innocent as the wild beasts pursue and devour the Hinds and Roes."[16]

Truth's account of the transit from Babel to Christendom also presents another metaphorical term that often appears in contrast to "wilderness" in *The Bloudy Tenent:* the garden, which symbolizes the church that genuinely follows the *"Ordinances* and *Discipline* of *Christ Jesus"* proclaimed in the New Testament, ordinances "the shining brightness of the very shadow" of which "casts a shame upon *barbarism* and *incivility."* Early in the book, Peace celebrates those believers who have tried to be good gardeners, so to speak: "You know some excellent *Worthies* (dead and living) have labored to turn this *Field* of the *World* into the *Garden* of the *Church."* Yet, like the Garden of Eden, the garden of the primitive church is no longer to be found or entered at the present day, for by their intervention in religious matters the rulers of the world have transformed it into a wilderness: "in spiritual things," Truth says, "they make the *Garden* and the *Wilderness* (as often I have intimated) I say the *Garden* and the *Wilderness,* the *Church* and the *World* are all one." The confusion runs more than one way: not only have these rulers made the garden into a wilderness, but they operate under the pretense that the wilderness is in fact a garden. Truth asks with withering irony,

> if the *Roman Emperors* were charged by *Christ* with his *Worship* in their dominion, and their *dominion* was over the *world* . . . who sees not if the whole world be forced to turn *Christian* (as afterward and since it hath pretended to do) then that the world (for whom Christ Jesus would not pray) and the *God* of it, are reconciled to *Jesus Christ,* and the whole *field* of the world become his enclosed *garden*?[17]

The ambiguity of "his," a pronoun that might refer back to either Christ or the "God" of this world, only emphasizes Williams's point: the notion of an enclosed garden (and a church congregation) as large as the world is nonsensical in a world that, as far as Williams is concerned, is still under the imperial aegis of Rome, with the Pope standing in for Caesar.

The *"Garden* and the *Wilderness* . . . are all one"—which is to say that the witness in the wilderness is also the witness *to* the wilderness, bearing the news that in this world there is no walled garden where believers can shelter themselves from desolation: "But now the partition *wall* is broken down, and in respect of the *Lords* special propriety to one Country more than another, what difference between *Asia* and *Africa,* between *Europe* and *America,* between *England* and *Turkey, London* and *Constantinople?"* The wilderness, as it happens, is a strikingly cosmopolitan (rather than metropolitan) place, in which the rigorous distinctions between peoples and places have "broken down." For this very reason the collapse of the garden into the wilderness, "taking away the difference between *Nation* and *Nation, Country* and *Country,"* does not turn Williams into a doomsayer, since that collapse is illustrating a point that should have been obvious to seekers after truth all along: "Are not all the *Nations* of the *Earth* alike clean unto *God,* or rather alike unclean, until it pleaseth the *Father* of *mercies* to call some out to the *Knowledge* and *Grace* of his *Son*[?]" After Christ's resurrection, there is no garden that receives his special favor and cultivation, but instead a universal wilderness replete with potential believers:

> But such a typical respect we find not now upon any People, *Nation* or *Country* of the whole *World:* But out of all *Nations, Tongues* and *Languages* is *God* pleased to call some and redeem them to Himself . . . [a]nd hath made no difference between the *Jews* and *Gentiles, Greeks* and *Scythians.*[18]

The contrast between Greeks and Scythians makes clear what is often muted in the familiar contrast between Jews and Gentiles: that God does not distinguish between the civil and the barbarous in summoning people to belief.

Here Williams draws upon both the language and argument of the Letter to the Romans, where early on Paul declares that "I am a debtor both to the Greeks, and to the Barbarians; both to the wise and unwise," and in which Paul's central assertions are that "there is no respect of persons with God" and "all have sinned, and come short of the glory of God" (Romans 1:14, 2:11, 3:23; see also Romans 3:9 and 10:12, and Galatians

3:28).[19] The Letter to the Romans is never far from Williams's mind as he prepares *The Bloudy Tenent;* in chapter 16, for instance, Williams borrows Paul's metaphor of the wild olive branch grafted into the "good" olive tree from Romans 11, once again in order to attack the efforts of Cotton and the leaders of the Bay Colony to impose their vision of the ecclesiastical garden upon the civil and secular wilderness:

> As if because *briars, thorns,* and *thistles* may not be in the *Garden* of the *Church,* therefore they must all be plucked up out of the *Wilderness:* whereas he that is a *Briar,* that is, a *Jew,* a *Turk,* a *Pagan,* an *Antichristian* to day, may be (when the Word of the *Lord* runs freely) a member of *Jesus Christ* to morrow cut out of the wild *Olive,* and planted into the true.

What bears stressing in this passage is its provisional character; the time "when the Word of the *Lord* runs freely" is part of a conditional future, and the transformation of the briar into a member of Christ's body is a possibility rather than fact. This state of potentiality calls for a particular sort of acceptance on the part of the believer. Just previously in the text, Truth has responded to Cotton's assertion that minor differences of doctrine and practice can and should be tolerated; this only leads Truth to broaden the field:

> [I]ndeed this is the very *ground* why the *Apostle* calls for meekness and gentleness toward *all* men, and toward such as oppose themselves . . . because there is a *peradventure* or *it may be;* It *may be* God may give them *Repentance.* That God that hath shown *mercy* to one, may show *mercy* to another: It may be that *eye-salve* that anointed *one mans* eye who was *blind* and opposite, may anoint another as *blind* and opposite.

The wilderness, one might say, is a field of possibility, of "a *peradventure* or *it may be,"* and as such it provides the field for Williams's broad (and, over the course of his writing career, broadly consistent) argument for freeing religious belief from the control of civil authority. For, in the wilderness of the world, one must recognize the possibility that all forms of such authority are equally valid: Truth asks, "who doubts but *Gods people* may appeal to the Roman *Caesar,* an Egyptian *Pharaoh,* a Philistian *Abimeleck,* an Assyrian *Nebuchadnezzar,* the great *Mogul, Prester John,* or an

Indian *Sachem?*"[20] The list appears to culminate in increasing levels of improbability as far as an Anglo-American "subject" would be concerned, moving from a Muslim emperor to an apocryphal Christian ruler (whose kingdom had wandered in Medieval and Renaissance geography from central Asia to central Africa, and whose existence was treated with growing skepticism by the mid-seventeenth century) and, finally, to a Native American chieftain. The sachem, then, is the ultimate benchmark in the passage; yet Williams declares him as legitimate a ruler as Caesar—or, by implication, the Bay magistrates.

Peace, in one of her longer replies to Truth in *The Bloudy Tenent,* remarks in chapter 6 that this functional equivalence of everything in the civil world offers no pressing occasion for spiritual judgment:

> Hence it is that so many glorious and flourishing Cities of the World maintain their *Civil* peace, yet the very *Americans* [i.e., Indians] & wildest *Pagans* keep the peace of their *Towns* or *Cities;* though neither in one nor the other can any man prove a true *Church* of God in those places, and consequently no spiritual and heavenly peace: The Peace *spiritual* (whether true or false) being of a higher and far different nature from the Peace of the place or people, being merely and essentially *civil* and *humane.*

This excursus—Peace speaking to peace, as it were—has a more pointed counterpart much later in the book, where Williams pushes the idea of the legitimacy of Native American government and Native American authority in the wilderness to its logical limit. The passage appears as part of Williams's point-by-point response, taking up most of the second half of *The Bloudy Tenent,* to "A Model of Church and Civil Power," a tract composed by Cotton and other Bay ministers in 1635 in defense of their efforts to rein in Williams and the Salem church at that time. Here Williams takes the claim of the authors of the "Model" that the authority of the magistrates reflects the will of the people (thus justifying persecution of those who disrupt the consensus) and drags it, figuratively if not literally, into the wilderness:

> It cannot by their own *Grant* be denied, but that the *wildest Indians* in *America* ought (and in their kind and several degrees do) to agree upon

some *forms* of *Government,* some more *civil,* compact in Townes, &c. some less. As also that their *civil* and *earthly Governments* be as lawful and true as any *Governments* in the *World,* and therefore consequently their *Governors* are *Keepers* of the *Church* or both *Tables,* (if any church of Christ should arise or be amongst them:) and therefore lastly, (if *Christ* have betrusted and charged the *civil* Power with his *Church*) they must judge according to their *Indian* or *American consciences,* for other *consciences* it cannot be supposed they should have.[21]

The Indians here represent not so much a reductio ad absurdum as a statement of Williams's argument in its most "naked" form: no magistrate, whatever his social milieu, has more right than any other to "keep both tables," to administer the religious as well as the civil ordinances in the Ten Commandments.

Peace's speech also offers some intriguing corollaries. The Indians inhabit a realm of potentiality, where certain things could happen, though they have not happened yet. In the first set of parentheses, a colon is placed strangely at the end of the clause—possibly just due to a typesetter's error, but also suggesting a literally open-ended sentence, holding out the prospect that there is something yet to be said, a potentiality still to be realized. Alongside this prospect, Williams posits the existence of *"Indian* or *American* consciences." A reader's initial impression may be that Williams is denigrating such consciences as being inferior to the European variety, but the overall tenor of the argument of *The Bloudy Tenent* leads toward another interpretation. In the wilderness of the world there are no enlightened consciences, but only consciences capable, to greater or lesser degrees, of being enlightened; in the wilderness, everyone has an American conscience.

The interpretations of the meaning of "the American wilderness" are beyond counting at this point, but in general they rely on a sort of sliding scale of metaphysical plenitude—from an awful emptiness or chaos, deprived of meaning, to an awesome treasury of moral and spiritual goods. Williams's concern with that wilderness, on the other hand, seems to lie elsewhere than in the realm of metaphysics: its value, at least for the purposes of an argument like the one in *The Bloudy Tenent,* is in its mimetic quality, its capacity for mirroring the world-at-large. The wilderness of New England is a microcosm of a universal wilderness, which is as much as to say of a universal equivalence. This wilderness, whether microcosm or macrocosm, is neither empty nor full of meaning; it is one where—except for the central historical moments of Christ's birth, death, and resurrection, and the scriptural record of those moments—almost anything is as meaningful (not, I want to emphasize, as meaningless) as any other thing. The world at large, as Williams presents it, is mired in postlapsarian mediocrity, a mediocrity that may be spiritually distasteful (for the world has indeed proven to be a world of sinners) but is, in practical terms, not unendurable. It is the wilderness that one lives in, and must live in.

Williams's understanding here has the paradoxical quality of seeming founded on the bedrock certainty of Scripture (this is what, he implies, Christ told us the world would be like), while opening the way toward a deeply radical pluralism; the combination would help to account for the immense distress that Williams caused to the church fathers in Boston, Salem, and Plymouth. His "pluralism," as such, rarely takes on a positive ideological form—he never offers a program for integrating Native Americans and English into a single polity, for instance—but it is significant in a broader cognitive dimension; in other words, it shapes the way that Williams thinks, and the kinds of matters he is able to think about.

Among the matters he can think about are the language, society, and culture of the Narragansetts—or, more precisely, their language, society, and culture as valid categories of inquiry. The value of the inquiry is not primarily that it will lead the Native Americans to Christianity; Williams believes that all conversions must be inward, so the most that the missionary can do is provide a range of materials to which individual souls can respond as they are moved to do so. Nor is it either to celebrate the innocence and "natural" virtue of Native Americans or to denigrate their savagery; broadly speaking, their moral character is not at issue. In the world-wilderness, as Williams describes it, civility is a matter of degree: to the extent that the Native Americans can arrange themselves in societies and govern themselves (as Williams acknowledges they can in fact do), they are civil. Therefore, they share a basic identity with other civil peoples, an identity that Williams understands as synchronic rather than diachronic: he is not interested in treating them merely as survivors of an original, prehistoric human order. As much as any other people, they are participants in the unfolding of the divine will in history; the distinct advantage they have over other peoples, as far as Williams is concerned, is that they are more readily observed—not only because they are close at hand, but also because their customs and activities are yet to be hedged in and crusted over with the accretions of Old World cultural and religious life. The hand of the Antichrist rests less heavily on them, and they are naked in the sense that (in New England, at least) they have never worn the papal robes. Williams treats the relative simplicity of Native American life not sentimentally but experimentally; to engage with that life is, so to speak, to have a "clean lab" in which to study God's plan being acted out in the wilderness—that is, in the human plane. It is not completely anachronistic, then, to say that Williams's engagement with the Narragansetts is anthropological, even though its motivation is ultimately theological. One of the guiding premises of anthropology (prior to Clifford Geertz and Marshall Sahlins, in any case) has been that by observing a particular society, one can extract structural principles that would apply to human societies in general. Williams employs a similar premise in a largely prescientific, nonsecular fashion: the witness in the wilderness describes the nature of humankind.

"Some Helps This Way": The Use of
A Key into the Language of America

I have canvassed *The Bloudy Tenent* at considerable length because I believe its premises and arguments help in an effort to "read back" to the ground and intent of *Key into the Language,* surely among the most unusual texts to emerge from colonial Anglo-America, apart from its distinctiveness within Williams's own corpus. A glossary, a guidebook, a controversialist tract, an anthology of poems, a defense of Native American culture, a scholarly inquiry, a personal testimony: *Key into the Language* is all of these things, yet each by itself is insufficient to account for the book as a whole. It is genuinely unique, and not only "in its projection of a developing relationship with the indigenous populations" of North America. As Ivy Schweitzer has noted, "There are literary historical precedents for the structural elements in the *Key,* but their combination and interrelation defy generic classification." Anne G. Myles suggests that Williams's authorial voice in *Key into the Language* is equally unclassifiable:

Williams refuses to be pinned down to a single location among the multiple sites he can occupy as humanistic New World observer, sincere
Protestant Englishman, disaffected cultural critic, and separatist Elijah.
Likewise, it is difficult to reach a single, stable conclusion about what he
achieved in his work.[22]

Key into the Language thus provides a "key" instance of a work that sits
uneasily on the shelf labeled American Literature (or perhaps simply
Literature) while at the same time inviting, if not requiring, literary
methods of interpretation.

As is often the case with works that have been neglected for a long period of time and then revisited during some larger shift of cultural attention (here, the postmodern revival of critical interest in early colonial
texts), *Key into the Language* now tends to be upheld as literature, as "a
Puritan work of art," with the coherence and continuity, both structural
and ideological, that such a phrase implies. This thread of argument runs
through Schweitzer's reading of the book. While her discussion clearly
shows the "de-authorizing" influence of new historicism and cultural
studies, she still finds in the connections between the book's poetry and
its other components the signs of a unified and controlling, though not
necessarily fully conscious, aesthetic vision: "the *Key* unerringly, perhaps
unintentionally, demonstrates . . . racial and religious limitations in its
blistering presentation of so-called civilized and Christian morality," a
presentation that depends on, among other things, "Williams's strategic
handling of allegory." Following in Schweitzer's wake, Thomas Scanlan
argues that "the narrative of the [Providence] colony was an allegory of
the narrative of the nation," by which he means the narrative of the
struggle for a reformed polity within England itself:

> Williams brilliantly and relentlessly frames his representations of In-
> dians by allowing his readers to see the extent to which they functioned
> as versions of themselves and their struggles. While appearing to bring
> home linguistic exotica, Williams in fact tacitly forces his readers to sit-
> uate issues of colonial rule in a domestic context.

Schweitzer's and Scanlan's accounts of *Key into the Language* both move
toward the notion of the book as a critique, even a satire, of the Massa-

chusetts Puritans' conviction of their intrinsic superiority to Native Americans.[23]

The element of critique is certainly present in *Key into the Language,* but in quite literal and transparent ways; it would be hard to miss the fact that in his poems and observations Williams regularly inverts the assumed moral positions of Native Americans and colonists and rarely hesitates to puncture the bubble of Puritan complacency. The simple point to make here is that Williams is not concealing this aspect of his intent in writing the book. Moreover, when one understands *Key into the Language* as belonging to the same mental universe as *The Bloudy Tenent,* portrayals of Williams as either an artful or artless allegorist begin to seem much less compelling—figures of Peace and Truth notwithstanding.[24] While Scanlan is at least partly right to say that *Key into the Language* posits an identification between Native Americans and colonists, this identification occurs in Williams's thought at a very generalized level: the Narragansetts represent a particular variant of the human condition, and so do the Puritans (so, for that matter, does any other society on earth). If allegory is a matter of figurative "arrows" pointing from one series of things to another, then the "arrows" in *Key into the Language* do not point consistently enough in a single direction to make for a coherent allegorical narrative. Williams certainly does compare the Narragansetts with the colonists—especially in the volume's poems, where he treats the similarities and differences emblematically—but comparisons do not an allegory make; one could argue that by being so explicit they are actually antithetical to allegory.

Of course one can always appeal to other definitions of art, such as the rhetorical "art" of *dispositio*—finding an appropriate arrangement for what might otherwise be merely a jumbled collection of facts and ideas. In *Key into the Language*'s famous prefatory letter, Williams is clearly aware of the need to impose order on his knowledge of the Narragansetts and their language:

> I drew the *Materials* in a rude lump at Sea, as a private *help* to my own memory, that I might not by my present absence *lightly lose* what I had so *dearly bought* in some few years *hardship,* and *charges* among the *Barbarians;* yet being reminded by some, what pity it were to bury those *Materials* in my *Grave* at land or Sea; and withal, remembering how oft I

have been importun'd by *worthy friends,* of all sorts, to afford them some helps this way.

I resolved (by the assistance of *the most High*) to cast those *Materials* into this *Key, pleasant* and *profitable* for *All,* but specially for my *friends* residing in those parts.[25]

This account of the book's genesis suggests little interest on Williams's part in promoting his book as an allegory of the sort that Scanlan and Schweitzer have in mind, in which an implicit narrative functions as critique, satire, or veiled autobiography. Williams's stated purposes are practical and didactic in a mode thoroughly familiar to writers and readers alike in the seventeenth century: *Key into the Language* is a mnemonic tool, a *"help* to my own memory" as well as the memories of others, especially of Williams's *"worthy friends";* it is a repository of distinctive and valuable knowledge (here Williams slips easily into comparing his knowledge to a vendible commodity, having *"dearly bought"* it); and it is educational, following the formula—as old at least as Aristotle—that knowledge should be both *"pleasant* and *profitable"* to its recipients.

This does not preclude talking about the aesthetic dimensions of *Key into the Language* (and I recognize the perils of taking authorial statements of purpose at face value in any case), but Williams's remarks in the prefatory letter do open the way for arguing that the volume is best illuminated less as a work of art that tilts toward allegory than as a technical project with a significant theological dimension. As such it participates in one of the characteristic modes of writing in Puritan communities, but a mode much easier to recognize when the writing involves "typically" Puritan topoi—the interpretation of the New Testament, the commemoration of divine providence, the self-examination of the soul. The emphasis is on spiritual and intellectual utility and the prospects for practical application; there is little or no sense that the work will be recognized and celebrated as "art" or generate an aesthetic response. Indeed, artifice might stand in the way of utility: rhetorical ornaments and elaborate conceits could easily distract from what would be most worth committing to memory in the text. This points to a problem with the effort of John J. Teunissen and Evelyn J. Hinz to align *Key into the Language* with the tradition of the emblem in seventeenth-century poetry and visual culture; to do so ignores the ubiquitous Puritan suspicion of imagery as the path to idolatry and, at the least, a clog to right thinking. As my former student James Atkinson has observed in a fine discussion of Williams, "It bears repeating here that Williams was a deeply and conservatively religious man both in outlook and in practice, and that it is unlikely that he would adopt what essentially is a popular and non-scriptural form to carry a fundamentally religious message."[26]

That *Key into the Language* contains a significant amount of poetry would appear to lead to quite a different conclusion about Williams's intentions, but even this feature of the text recalls, and participates in, a venerable didactic tradition: the Latin textbooks of the Middle Ages, for example, frequently included pieces of verse that served to summarize or reinforce the material under discussion. What initially registers as a form of eccentric ornamentation in Williams's book might instead support the idea, argued so forcefully by Miller early in *The New England Mind,* that "the settlers of New England retained with few alterations the cosmology of the Middle Ages, even though they constantly denounced its authors."[27]

In his specific assessments of Williams, Miller offers what remains a sensibly cautionary approach to examining the question of Williams's aesthetics. Arguing that Williams treats the Old Testament as "figurative," "a work of the imagination," and "not historical" but "dramatic," Miller concludes:

> To put this emphasis upon Williams is to employ terms used in literary criticism. But Williams . . . was no theorist of the "creative" mind. He could not have conceived of the Bible "as literature," a twentieth-century notion. He was a Calvinist theologian endeavoring to frame anew the issue between the individual conscience and authority in a post-Reformation world. Yet he does appertain to what modern scholars call the literary or at least symbolizing turn of mind, rather than the historical. He advocated the apprehended meaning, disregarding archaeological and philological interpretations in their historical context.[28]

The last part of this comment needs, I think, some qualification. It arises from Miller's rather overwrought reading of Williams as a typologist (discussed further in the Appendix) and implies that Williams's approach to hermeneutics is much more idiosyncratic and his disregard for historical context more extensive than is actually the case. Yet Miller is right to stress the importance of personal apprehension in Williams's interpretive model, where the judgment of the individual conscience always takes precedence over judgments emanating from institutional authority or public consensus. Insofar as a work like *Key into the Language* has a literary cast, it is surely related to Williams's unabashed presentation of his work as the product of an individual conscience: a book, one would say, possessed—and reflective—of a distinct personality.

An interesting ambiguity surrounds Williams's celebration of the solitary conscience and its powers, however: while this conscience, when touched by grace, is capable of great feats of intellectual and spiritual discernment (and, one supposes, artistic expression), it is also capable of severe misapprehension and misjudgment. As Peace says, more or less proverbially, in *The Bloudy Tenent*, "*Satan* useth excellent *arrows* to bad *marks,* and sometimes beyond the *intent,* and hidden from the eye of the *Archer.*"[29] The human mind is, after all, a fallen mind, and Williams's sharp awareness of that mind's capacity for error (sharper, if that seems possible, than that of many of his intellectual contemporaries in the Bay Colony) leads in *Key into the Language* to a highly unusual mode of presentation, especially in the Puritan context. Efforts to sort out the peculiarity of the book in aesthetic terms may have the effect of obscuring its methodological peculiarity. What finally makes it a rarity is that it is speculative in a very different manner than most of the intellectual projects that originate out of seventeenth-century New England.

With this claim in mind, I want to return to the idea that Williams intends his book to be a "help," both private and public: "for want of this [key], I know not what gross *mis-takes* my self and others have run into." The text will help to forestall error, will prevent its readers from getting lost (for this appears to be the underlying metaphor) in "those *Countries,* where ever *English* dwell about two hundred miles, between the *French* and *Dutch* plantations." To the various contemporary meanings of the word "key" that critics have educed relative to this book, it is important to add a sense of the key as an instrumental aid—something that allows one to do other things, such as enter a particular space. This may serve at least partly to explain Williams's famously cryptic statement, "A little *Key* may open a *Box,* where lies a *bunch* of *Keys.*" With this little key Williams has "entered into the secrets" of the land where not only the English dwell but also the language of America is spoken. With this little key, the various filiations of the Algonquian language in New England will potentially open themselves to the reader: "within the two hundred miles (aforementioned) their *Dialects* do exceedingly differ; yet not so, but (within that compass) a man may, by this *help,* converse with *thousands* of *Natives* all over the *Country.*"[30]

Thus *Key into the Language* is a tool that, like a lever or pulley, efficiently multiplies the force of individual effort. The ability to "converse" (here Williams seems to play interestingly on the kinship between "conversation" and "conversion") is powerfully expansive, if not expansionist, since

> by such converse it may please the *Father* of *Mercies* to spread *civility,* (and in his own most holy season) *Christianity;* for *one Candle* will light *ten thousand,* and it may please *God* to bless a *little Leaven* to season the *mighty Lump* of those *Peoples* and *Territories.*

The passage makes clear that *Key into the Language* is a form of agency available to those few who will be preparing the way for the arrival of the Gospel onto what has been, linguistically if not geographically, an uncertain frontier. This *"mighty Lump"* is, in any case, the sum of several parts, existing in both social and physical dimensions *("Peoples* and *Territories").* As several scholars have noted, the last sentence in the passage alludes to the parable, recounted in both Matthew 13:33 and Luke 13:21–22, in which Christ compares the kingdom of heaven to a woman who concealed leaven in three measures of flour, so that all the flour became, to use Williams's term, "season[ed]."[31] *Key into the Language,* then, does have an unambiguous purpose: it assists in laying the groundwork for the raising of the kingdom of God on earth, a kingdom that will rise with the assistance of the particular leaven of an ability to have "converse" with the peoples who compose a major portion of the "mighty Lump."

What remains ambiguous, however, is the schedule for this most momentous event. On this question, Williams's expression becomes conditional, tentative: "it may please" God (in his own "season"—and the noun "season" produces a curious discord with the same word used as a verb a little later) to civilize and convert the Native Americans, to bless the leaven. Williams offers a somewhat more optimistic formulation at the end of the introduction; promising an "Additional discourse" on the project of conversion (a text that Teunissen and Hinz identify with the pamphlet *Christenings Make Not Christians,* printed in 1645), Williams claims to be

> comfortably persuaded that that Father of Spirits, who was graciously pleased to persuade *Japhet* (the Gentiles) to dwell in the Tents of *Shem* (the Jews) will in his holy season (I hope approaching) persuade these Gentiles of *America* to partake of the mercies of *Europe,* and then shall be fulfilled what is written, by the Prophet *Malachi,* from the rising of the Sun (in *Europe*) to the going down of the same (in *America*) my Name shall [be] great among the Gentiles.

Williams is quite explicit about his desideratum here: it is the global unification of gentiles under God, fulfilling the words of the prophet in a way that Europeans could not have guessed prior to 1492. But while one can now understand what the "holy season" might be like, one cannot predict its actual arrival.[32]

At one level, Williams is simply being a strict biblical literalist; for example, in the first chapter of Acts, Christ, appearing to the disciples after his resurrection, responds to their most pressing question: "they asked of him, saying, 'Lord, wilt thou at this time restore again the kingdom to Israel?' And he said unto them, 'It is not for you to know the times or the seasons, which the father hath put in his own power'" (Acts 1:6–7; see also Matthew 24:36–44 and Mark 13:32–37). But Williams also implicitly acknowledges the futility of any human effort to raise God's kingdom; people can offer themselves (or the fruits of their labor) as instruments toward achieving a desired outcome and yet have no immediate expectation of seeing that outcome achieved. This mitigates what readers might see as the boldness of Williams's subsequent remark, in which he appears to identify himself logically with the *"one candle"* and the *"little leaven"*: "It is expected, that having had so much converse with these *Natives,* I should write some little of them."[33]

The problem that Williams faces in the preface to *Key into the Language,* and that I have suggested is just as present in *The Bloudy Tenent,* has to do with unknowability—not only the ultimate unknowability of God's "holy season," but also the contingent unknowability of the Narragansetts as possible converts to Christianity. Throughout these early pages, Williams struggles against an urge to speak definitively about the condition of

Native American souls: "Other opinions I could number up: under favor I shall present (not mine opinion, but) my *Observations* to the judgment of the Wise." Yet observation only takes Williams so far. He cannot speak authoritatively about origins of the Native American peoples of New England, beyond the origin that they share with everyone else in the world:

> From *Adam* and *Noah* that they spring, it is granted on all hands.
> But for their later *Descent,* and whence they came into those parts, it seems as hard to find, as to find the *Wellhead* of some fresh *Stream,* which running many miles out of the *Country* to the salt *Ocean,* hath met with many mixing *Streams* by the way. They say themselves, that they have *sprung* and *grown* up in that very place, like the very *trees* of the *Wilderness.*

It is characteristic of Williams's approach in *Key into the Language* that the only further version of *"Descent"* he offers is the Narragansetts' own—and that he says nothing more about it. Commenting a little later on the Narragansetts' tendency to assign spiritual powers to the southwest quadrant of the world, he notes that the tribe's crops grow better toward that direction, but then stops himself: "I dare not conjecture in these *Uncertainties,* I believe they [the Narragansetts] are *lost,* and yet hope (in the Lords holy season) some of the wildest of them shall be found to share in the blood of the Son of God." Turning "to that great point of their *Conversion* so much to be longed for," Williams enumerates the traits that he knows are signs of readiness, but again brings himself up short upon the (crucial) place where his knowledge fails:

> I know there is no small *preparation* in the hearts of Multitudes of them.
> I know their many solemn *Confessions* to my self, and one to another of their lost *wandering Conditions.*
> I know strong *Convictions* upon the *Consciences* of many of them, and their desires uttered that way.
> I know not with how little *Knowledge* and *Grace* of Christ, the Lord may save, and therefore neither will *despair,* nor *report* much.[34]

The alliterative pull of confessions, conditions, convictions, and consciences seems to lead Williams toward a certainty that he finally refuses, faced with the intertwined problems of knowledge and grace. What

Williams knows about the Narragansetts at the personal level is simply not sufficient to answer larger questions of soteriology.

This diffidence, interestingly enough, frees up the language and culture of the Narragansetts as objects of investigation beyond the categories of Protestant dogma (or, to put it another way, it frees Williams to write about the Narragansetts as having not only a language but also a culture). They, no less than the Puritans, share in the progress of God's cosmic plan; unlike the Puritans, however, they are encountering that plan in its full dimensions for the first time. This does not make them prelapsarian innocents, but it does place them closer to the first-century peoples from which the earliest converts to Christianity were drawn. The sense of their analogical relation to historically specific pre-Christian communities may help to account for Williams's apparently contradictory effort in the introduction to find both Hebrew and Greek antecedents for the Narragansetts and their language. To move among them and transact business with them is like being in Palestine at the moment when Christ began preaching, or in Asia Minor at the outset of Paul's missionary journeys. Whoever uses *Key into the Language* is carrying it across the threshold of the history of salvation. Williams would argue that almost all Christian communities stand on the same threshold; their understanding of their true position is obscured, however, by their confidence that they have passed over it and are well on their way toward the ultimate goal. The Native American communities have no such presumptions: "they will say, We never heard of this before."[35] Thus, for Williams and the putative reader of *Key into the Language,* the Narragansetts present an opportunity to observe, in as close to an unmediated fashion as one is likely to find, the ways that God works his purpose out at the most basic levels of the human condition.

This does not necessarily mean that one draws definite conclusions from what one observes; but (given what is at stake) one is very careful to make good observations, to distinguish precisely between different things, to identify what one can identify within one's lights. *Key into the Language* might best be understood as a manual for "fieldwork," though of neither a strictly ethnographic nor a strictly missionary sort. With the inclusion of various aids to memory and judgment (not least of which are its topical poems), Williams's book offers, as it were, a taxonomic and diagnostic guide—a key!—to the effect of God's providence on "American consciences."[36]

One Blood: The Narragansetts as Exemplars

It makes sense, then, that the word lists in *Key into the Language* lean heavily toward the language of commonplace social exchanges—"not official language," as Myles puts it, "but practical and secular speech, that which is spoken by individuals"[37]—and that the commentary so frequently relies on anecdotes about Williams's face-to-face encounters with the Narragansetts. He is deeply interested in the moment when the matter of revelation is introduced into ordinary conversation among people with little or no knowledge of the Gospel. For him this moment has a near-universal validity; it is the moment when the conversion of any unbeliever begins. Williams is much less exacting about where the process ends. The anecdotes tend not to resolve very clearly. In the introduction, for example, there is the account of Williams's conversation with Wequash, a Pequot, just before Wequash's death. After Williams "acquainted him with the Condition of all mankind, & his Own in particular," Wequash responds with austere eloquence:

> said he *your words were never out of my heart to this present;* and said he *me much pray to Jesus Christ:* I told him so did many *English, French,* and *Dutch,* who had never turned to *God,* nor loved him: He replied in broken English: *Me so big naughty Heart, me heart all one stone! Savory expressions* using to breath *from compunct and broken hearts,* and a sense of *inward hardness* and *unbrokenness.*

Has Williams, then, "broken" through Wequash's heart? Has a successful conversion taken place? Williams does not say, most likely because he does not know. His reply to Wequash, that many "Christians" pray without being sanctified, is hardly reassuring. He concludes, "this was the sum of our last parting until our general meeting"—a meeting on the Day of Judgment, where those assembled will have yet another "parting," to two entirely different destinations.[38]

Other anecdotes are similarly inconclusive. In chapter 8, "Of *Discourse and News,*" Williams appends the following "Observation" to the

Narragansett expression "Michéme nipannowâutam" *("I shall never believe it"):* "As one answered me when I had discoursed about many points of God . . . he assented; but when I spake of the rising again of the body, he cried out, I shall never believe this." This is the extent of the remark; Williams does not indicate whether the disbelief was ever overcome. Several such passages can be found in the long and, as many readers would say, climactic chapter 21, *"Of religion, the soul, &c."* In this chapter, Williams notoriously presents a kind of script for initiating conversions among the Narragansetts:

> Now because this Book (by Gods good providence) may come into the hand of many fearing God, who may also have many an opportunity of occasional discourse with some of these their wild brethren and Sisters, and may speak a word for their and our glorious Maker, which may also prove some preparatory Mercy to their Souls: I shall propose some proper expressions . . . which who knows (in Gods holy season) may rise to exalting of the Lord Jesus Christ in their conversion, and salvation?

Some of the rhetorical tics in this passage should be familiar by now: the proliferation of the auxiliary verb "may," the parenthetical qualifiers, the statement that finally grades into a question. The glossary that follows, mostly a digest of the first chapter of Genesis, has one noticeably open-ended moment, involving an ambiguity about the number and identity of the interlocutors in the "script."

Tasuóg Maníttowock?	*How many Gods be there?*
Maunaúog Mishaúnowock	*Many, great many.*
Nétop machàge.	*Friend, not so.*
Paúsuck naúnt manìt.	*There is only one God.*
Cuppíssittone.	*You are mistaken.*
Cowauwaúnemun.	*You are out of the way.*

> A phrase which much pleaseth them, being proper for their wandering in the woods, and similitudes greatly please them.

"Cuppíssittone" and "Cowauwaúnemun" could be spoken equally readily by a colonist or a Narragansett, but Williams leaves the reader to conjecture who is repudiating whom—making his subsequent allusion to "wandering in the woods" seem particularly apt.[39]

The script moves on to a shorthand account of heaven and hell, which concludes with an appeal to scriptural authority:

Wame naûmakiaûog.	*They [i.e., sinners] go to Hell or*
	the Deep.
Micheme maûog.	*They shall ever lament.*
Awaun kukkakotemógwunnes?	*Who told you so?*
Manittóo wússuckwheke.	*Gods Book or Writing.*

In the observation that follows from this, Williams tells a rather murky tale about one of his own evangelical encounters, involving the Narragansett chieftain Miantonomi:

A *Qunníhticut* Indian (who had heard our discourse) told the *Sachem Miantunnómu,* that souls went [not] up to Heaven, or down to Hell; For, saith he, Our fathers have told us, that our souls go to the *Southwest.*

The *Sachem* answered, But how do you know your self, that your souls go to the *Southwest;* did you ever see a soul go thither?

The Native replied; when did he (naming my self) see a soul go to Heaven or Hell?

The *Sachem* again replied: He hath books and writings, and one which God himself made, concerning mens souls, and therefore may well know more than we that have none, but take all upon trust from our forefathers.[40]

At this point, Williams records that the topic of the discussion between Miantonomi and the Connecticut Indian shifted to the question of whether or not to observe the English sabbath, and Williams himself turns to defending his unwillingness to impose his own religious practices on the Narragansetts. He offers no reflections of any sort on the Connecticut's pointed questions about the afterlife or Miantanomi's somewhat evasive response. If there is a hidden irony in the sachem's distinction between one kind of conservative appeal to authority ("books and writings") and another ("our forefathers"), Williams neglects to elucidate it. He does not even indicate what, if anything, Miantonomi decided about the sabbath.

How does one account for Williams's lack of concern with extracting a moral from these exchanges, or even with ending his stories? A plausible answer to this question is, as I have implied above, that his concern actually lies elsewhere—on the frontier of conversion, so to speak, where Williams's method is usually descriptive rather than determinative. *Key into the Language* maps out the windings, obstacles, forks, side paths, and dead ends that occur on the narrow way that leads to the Second Coming. To understand with genuine precision how the process of salvation goes forward, Williams suggests, one must try to consider without either complacency or prejudice (and, by implication, free from the pressure of institutional authority) the raw elements that go into that process—and those elements, both the ones that help and the ones that hinder, are most readily accessible in simple acts of speech that are largely devoid of theological refinements. From this perspective, the speech of the Narragansetts can serve as a representation of human speech in general—the assumption being that not only a Narragansett is capable of saying, *"Me heart all one stone,"* or "I shall never believe this," or "When did he see a soul go to heaven or hell?" That such speech has not been thoroughly Christianized only makes it more useful for Williams's purposes; *Key into the Language* promotes an even plainer version of the "Plain Style."

The passage from language to lifeways is usually a short one—indeed the move from one to the other is the rationalizing principle of Williams's text—and the representativeness of Native American speech grades readily into the representativeness of Native American society. Williams is at pains throughout his commentary to emphasize the claim that he makes in chapter 7, "Of *their Persons* and *parts of body,*" that "Nature knows no difference between *Europe* and *Americans* in blood, birth, bodies, &c. God having of one blood made all mankind." The most obvious means of stressing this "one blood" is by comparing the Native Americans to the English, which Williams does frequently, especially in his concluding poems. But often the comparisons are to a generic category of European humanity, as in the observation on the Narragansetts' sophisticated mathematical skills in chapter 4 ("Let it be considered, whether *Tradition* of ancient *Forefathers,* or *Nature* hath taught them *Europes Arithmetic"*—tellingly, Williams offers two possible causes without preferring one to the other) or in chapter 6, *"Of the Family and business of the house,"* where Williams claims that the Narragansetts "are as full of business, and as impatient of hindrance (in their kind) as any Merchant in *Europe.*"[41]

Just as often, the comparisons are still more "global" in character. The

Narragansetts share in the universal fear of death—they "abhor to name the dead (Death being the King of Terrors to all natural men)"—and in the transhistorical love of getting the latest word: "Their desire of, and delight in news, is great, as the *Athenians,* and all men, more or less." They organize their communal and domestic lives as other peoples do:

> The sociableness of the nature of man appears in the wildest of them, who love society; Families, cohabitation, and consociation of houses and towns together.
>
> . . . .
>
> With friendly joining they break up their fields, build their Forts, hunt the Woods, stop and kill fish in the Rivers, it being true with them as in all the World in the Affairs of Earth or Heaven: By concord little things grow great, by discord the greatest come to nothing.
>
> . . . .
>
> The wildest of the sons of Men have found a necessity, (for preservation of themselves, their Families and Properties) to cast themselves into some mold or form of Government.
>
> . . . .
>
> God hath planted in the Hearts of the Wildest of the sons of Men, an High and Honorable esteem of the Marriage bed, insomuch as they universally submit unto it.

The Narragansetts also show the general human tendency to measure life by the heavens:

> The *Sun* and *Moon,* in the observation of all the *sons* of *men,* even the wildest, are the great *Directors* of the *day* and *night.*
>
> . . . .
>
> The *Sun* and *Moon,* and *Stars* and *seasons* of the year do preach a *God* to all the sons of men, that they which know no letters, do yet read an *eternal Power* and *Godhead* in these.
>
> . . . .
>
> The wildest sons of Men hear the preaching of the Heavens, the Sun, Moon, and Stars, yet not seeking after God the Maker are justly condemned.[42]

Most of the comments above occur as the culminating "General Observations" in the chapters in which they appear; *Key into the Language* is quite literally always leading up to the thesis that the Narragansetts are typical "sons of men" bearing the mark of original sin, thus "natural men" because they are inheritors of Adam's nature. They may be the "wildest" members of the category, but for Williams this is no disadvantage, since they exemplify in the starkest terms both the plight and the promise of the human race.

From the medial position where he places the Narragansetts in the wilderness of the world, Williams occasionally ventures out to test the edges. How far does God's grace actually extend? Is it indeed available even at the extremes of the human condition, or are believers in the habit of merely paying lip service to this notion? In touching on these questions, Williams turns not to the Narragansetts for his "limit cases" but to two remote tribes with a cultural affinity to one another (or very likely the same tribe under two different names). In chapter 2 he describes the Mihtukméchakick, the *"Tree-eaters,"*

> A people so called (living between three and four hundred miles West into the land) from their eating only *Mihtúchquash,* that is, Trees: They are *Men-eaters,* they set no corn, but live on the bark of *Chestnut* and *Walnut,* and other fine trees: They dry and eat this *bark* with the fat of Beasts, and sometimes of men: This people are the *terror* of the Neighbor *Natives;* and yet these *Rebels,* the Son of God may in time subdue.[43]

The strangeness of this tribe is marked by its sheer distance from Narragansett territory; yet its members, even with their seemingly inhuman diet, are not beyond the reach of the Gospel—nor, it is important to note, beyond Williams's capacity to think of them as being within reach.

Even more striking is Williams's reference to the Mauquaúogs in chapter 7, "Of *their Persons* and *parts of body,*" following from the gloss on "Wuttìp," *"The brain":*

> In the brain their [i.e., the Narragansetts'] opinion is, that the soul . . . keeps her chief seat and residence:
> For the temper of the brain in quick apprehensions and accurate judgments (to say no more) the most high and sovereign God and Creator, hath not made them inferior to *Europeans.*
> The *Mauquaúogs,* or *Men-eaters,* that live two or three [hundred] miles West from us, make a delicious monstrous dish of the head and brains

of their enemies; which yet is no bar (when the time shall approach) against Gods call, and their repentance, and (who knows but) a greater love to the Lord Jesus? great sinners forgiven love much.[44]

The effect of this passage depends on the rapid, even jarring shift from the celebration of the power of Native American reason to an account of what appears to be the antithesis of reason: a tribe that values "American consciences" mainly because they taste good. Williams himself seems to relish presenting this "delicious monstrous" dish in the text, at least in part because its shock value is meant to exercise the brains of his readers also. For the Mauquaúogs, no less than the Narragansetts, are capable of "quick apprehensions and accurate judgments"; they are typical rational creatures, just as fallen from grace and just as capable of redemption as any other "sinners," great or small. Their redemption may be approaching, though—as is usually the case—Williams is careful to phrase this idea in the form of a question rather than a claim, and to hedge it with parenthesized reservations. As he asks repeatedly in the text, both explicitly and implicitly, *who knows?*

The continuous presence of these intertwined elements in *Key into the Language*—the argument for the exemplary character of the Narragansetts and the rhetorically "soft" way in which Williams expresses that argument—brings me back to reflection on the general nature of the knowledge project embodied in the book and on the troublesome question of what Williams's gathering of knowledge about the Narragansetts finally amounts to. Is it possible to reconcile Williams's obvious (and for the period well-nigh unique) interest in the particulars of Native American culture with the fact that this interest is framed within an apocalyptic theological conception that is fundamentally, one might say cosmically, apathetic to those particulars? (Here one recalls Williams's famous refusal to "be an eye witness, Spectator, or looker on" at Narragansett religious ceremonies, "lest I should have been partaker of Satans Inventions and Worships.") In the recent criticism of *Key into the Language,* there has been considerable debate as to whether or not the Narragansetts simply disappear into the frame. Myles argues that "If we read it looking for traces of authentic indigenous presence or compare it to texts authored by Native Americans themselves, *A Key* falls painfully short," though she

goes on to say that "to produce such a work was never Williams's intention." Schweitzer concludes that the book embodies a struggle between
Williams's allegorical critique of the failings of his coreligionists and the
"finally 'irreducible' wordmass of the Narragansett tongue":

> the text attempts to subordinate the literal reality of the native world—
> which is also, after all, the world Williams enters, observes, and to a
> large extent shares—to the atemporal spiritual reality of scriptural alle-
> gory. The Narragansett become instrumental, mediating between
> Williams and God, Williams and his foes. Yet, his reductive efforts are
> not wholly successful.

Rubertone offers a more charitable interpretation, arguing from the
impossibility of recovering a comprehensive sense of Williams's relations
with the Narragansetts based on the surviving written records:

> In the absence of readily available answers and simple formulas, how is
> it possible to judge what Williams did not see or what he might not have
> recognized as important to those whose lives he attempted to repre-
> sent? By reading A Key closely, one can hear the voices of the Narra-
> gansett people. No amount of overwriting or imposed meanings based
> on existing preconceptions has obliterated them completely.[45]

From their rather different stances, these critics assume that *Key into the
Language* succeeds *against* itself. This may be so, but I think there is also
some value in reframing the picture. The theological ground of the work
is inescapable, and indeed there is no reason that present-day readers
should try to escape it, since in this respect it is of a piece not only with
The Bloudy Tenent but also with Williams's entire *opera*. But from this
ground emerges an investigation that is, for lack of a better word, phe-
nomenological in character. Where most Puritan writing looks for the
workings of Providence on familiar turf—in the community's historical
record of its own activities, in Scripture, in various renderings of personal
experience—Williams's field of inquiry is one that *resists* familiarity, that
cannot be readily assimilated to "common sense," to the normative assumptions of one's own culture.

Precisely because that field is resistant—"replete with an undeniable opacity," as Schweitzer puts it[46]—it is spiritually salutary. It removes the scales from one's eyes, so that one can see rightly the multiple, recondite, unanticipated, sometimes completely shocking ways that God acts in the quotidian and preeminently *social* space that Williams so often designates as a "wilderness" and that is, in a significant way, the space of language itself. Something of the same impulse led a writer and thinker like John Donne (who died in 1631, the year that Williams arrived in Massachusetts) to mine *his* language for the most distant and paradoxical metaphors in search of sacred truths. For Williams, the Narragansetts are intrinsically worth knowing because they speak a language quite unlike English, and the effort to make sense of it implies a broader education of the mind and soul in preparation for "God's holy season"—broader, in any case, than the education offered in the churches and schools of Massachusetts. It is true that in this view the Narragansetts remain a means to an end, a path by which an English witness may come to know the real meaning of the New Testament; but the pursuit of the end does not erase them from the picture, either by removing them or by transforming them from an indigenous society into another conventional Christian community. In a relatively positive sense, they still hold their ancestral lands within Williams's wilderness, which is to say a terrain with both physical and cognitive dimensions.

Wilderness and Mind

Míchachunck, the soul . . . which is of affinity, with a word signifying a looking glass, or clear resemblance, so that it hath its name from a clear sight or discerning, which indeed seems very well to suit with the nature of it.

—*Key into the Language,* chap. 21

I want to offer a final note on an issue that has been hovering on the periphery of my discussion of Williams; but of course there is no periphery without a center to help define it, and vice versa. In this chapter, and in fact throughout this book, I have studiously avoided elevating particular aspects of a text as being identifiably "American" in character, and as inaugurating or anticipating cultural developments that would come to fruition after the colonial era. Many critics and historians have pointed out the problems with a teleology in which colonial writers become ghostly forebears of red-blooded nineteenth-century thinkers.[47] I think it is appropriate, though, to say a few more words about an aspect of Williams's idea of wilderness, an aspect that is evident in both *The Bloudy Tenent* and *Key into the Language* and the traces of which are recognizable in so many later texts originating from or associated with North America. Whether that aspect originates with Williams or not is probably immaterial; what matters is that it at least exists in his work and thus becomes available for interpretation within the historical field.

In Williams's writing, wilderness is not the antithesis of civilization (civility being a matter of degree), nor the wellspring of pure nature (an impossibility in a fallen world); nor is it a place of pastoral retreat (for no one can retreat from the central problem of existence, which turns on one's relationship with God). It has rather too many inhabitants to provide much in the way of physical solitude. And it is no more divine or demonic than any other place in the world; as I have argued above, it *is* the world. Its one great benefit is that, because it is mostly empty of the customary institutions of European social, cultural, and religious life, it provides a space for thinking, and thinking of a particularly open-ended sort. There is a long tradition in Western culture in which one withdraws from civil society for the sake of the mind, to spend time in reflection and contemplation; but this withdrawal is nearly always tied to an eventual return to a familiar milieu. With Williams, this tie is broken; the thinker feels no pressing need to come back and is content merely to send the occasional message back to the bastions of civilization, since the only return that matters is Christ's at the end of the age. (I am speaking in symbolic terms here, of course, since Williams's career involved regular shuttling between the metropolis and the frontier.) Williams's books provide some of the earliest instances of an argument that, for better or worse, gradually rises to a prominent place among the multiple claims—cosmopolitan, reactionary, dissenting, conformist, mystical, pragmatic—that serve to form the intellectual culture of the colonies and the nation. The argument could be stated this way: the proper venue of the mind, where it performs its best work and "sees" most clearly into both spiritual and worldly things, is not an enclosed and civil garden but instead a terrain without fences, permanent structures, good roads, or tilled fields, where the next voice to be heard might ask, "Tocketunnântum?"—"*What think you?*"[48]

Conclusion

—ᘓᘓ—

Chains of Knowledge

For men have entered into a desire of learning and knowledge, sometimes upon a natural curiosity and inquisitive appetite; sometimes to entertain their minds with variety and delight; sometimes for ornament and reputation; and sometimes to enable them to victory of wit and contradiction; and most times for lucre and profession; and seldom sincerely to give a true account of their gift of reason, to the benefit and use of men: as if there were sought in knowledge a couch, whereupon to rest a searching and restless spirit; or a terrace, for a wandering and variable mind to walk up and down with a fair prospect; or a tower of state, for a proud mind to raise itself upon; or a fort and commanding ground, for strife and contention; or a shop, for profit or sale; and not a rich storehouse, for the glory of the Creator and relief of man's estate. But this is that which will indeed dignify and exalt knowledge, if contemplation and action may be more nearly and straitly conjoined and united together than they have been; a conjunction like unto that of the two highest planets, Saturn the planet of rest and contemplation, and Jupiter the planet of civil society and action.

—FRANCIS BACON, *The Advancement of Learning*

Everything that is set down in writing is to some extent foreign and strange, and hence it poses the same task of understanding as what is spoken in a foreign language. The interpreter of what is written, like the interpreter of divine or human utterance, has the task of overcoming and removing the strangeness and making its assimilation possible. It may be the case that this task is complicated if the historical distance between the text and interpreter becomes conscious; for this means that the tradition that supports both the transmitted text and its interpreter has become fragile and gapped.

—HANS-GEORG GADAMER, Supplement I to *Truth and Method*

> The work itself indeed is nothing more than the measure of a shadow, never stationary, but lengthening as the sun advances, and to be taken anew from hour to hour. It must remain, therefore, for some other hand to sketch its appearance at another epoch.
>
> —THOMAS JEFFERSON, letter to John Melish, December 10, 1814

I will close with some remarks on the reception history—the afterlife— of knowledge projects such as the ones I have discussed in this book. In my introduction and in the chapter on Smith, I broached the question of the reception of colonial texts in terms of literary and cultural criticism, but the question can be treated more broadly. What kinds of influence did the works of John Smith, William Bradford, Thomas Morton, and Roger Williams have on the way that subsequent generations came to know the North American colonial world? At first glance, the record seems mixed at best. *Of Plymouth Plantation,* especially its first book, has certainly helped to define the modern understanding of Plymouth Colony. Smith's writing has had a lasting if circumscribed impact; I am thinking here of the mythography of his encounter with Pocohontas, but it would be hard to extrapolate from that encounter a comprehensive interpretation of Native American life in tidewater Virginia. The influence of Williams is localized in a rather different way: while he is more or less generally under- stood to be the first major proponent of the separation of church and state in America, his *specific* accounts of the things that concerned him are rarely commemorated outside of Rhode Island and certain sectors of the Baptist faith. With Morton, the case is murky; perhaps there is still a ten- dency in some quarters to treat the activities of the Pilgrims and Puritans as more deserving of ridicule than serious consideration. But it would also be possible to claim that Morton's work produced merely a dim awareness over time that not every English settler in Massachusetts in the seventeenth century agreed with the message of "A Modell of Christian Charity."

One is inclined to say that the works of Smith, Bradford, Morton, and Williams dwindle into insignificance beside the seventeenth-century knowl- edge projects of, say, Francis Bacon, Isaac Newton, Thomas Hobbes, and John Locke, projects that have continued to the present day to affect the ways that we know the world around us, as well as the ways that we think about *how* we know that world. But this comparison obscures the crucial point, which is that such projects continue to function as long as they have readers who respond to them *as* knowledge projects (rather than as artifacts or curios, along the lines of the quaint newspaper articles and theater programs pulled out of reopened time capsules or displayed behind glass in historical museums). This was Thomas Jefferson's insight in writing to the publisher John Melish about the prospects for a revised edition of his *Notes on the State of Virginia*. He perceived that his work—a classic American knowledge project if there ever was one, but one that Jefferson viewed as fatally imperfect and incomplete—would come to fruition only when it was linked to someone else's similar project at some point in the future. Under this view, any knowledge project that does not fall completely out of circulation, as certainly many have, will survive and perhaps even thrive when it is taken up into a network of knowledge-making, a network that might develop at a remove of many years—even centuries—from the date of the original project. This is not to say that every individual knowledge project deserves to be brought back into circulation; many are self-serving, deluded, fraudulent, incompetent, politically manipulative, or irredeemably flawed in some logical or technical way. Some are downright dangerous, as persistent as they are pernicious (the theories of scientific racism, for example). Yet even the ugliest and most troublesome of such projects are always subject to reflection, interrogation, correction. The first volume of Perry Miller's *The New England Mind* and its close contemporary, William Haller's *The Rise of Puritanism,* are both instances of modern knowledge projects centered on the investigation of texts that most previous intellectual historians had found too tedious, hermetic, or otherwise forbidding for sustained inquiry. To turn to a more recent example, postcolonial criticism as a movement can be understood as an effort to retrieve the often repellent knowledge projects of European imperialism and place them under the gaze of contemporary knowers. Thus chains of knowledge are formed—not leading inevitably to truth, of course, but at least sustaining the process of trying to discover what in this world is true and what is not. If knowledge does indeed advance over time, this process of "generational" linking appears to me to be a primary way in which it does so.

The writers from the far Anglo-American past that have occupied my attention in this book may have failed to find broad readerships in their own time for the colonial knowledge they sought to promulgate, yet they all wrote in the expectation that somewhere there existed an eagerness, a hunger, for what they had to offer, that their projects would find "lovers of all good knowledge," to recur to John Frampton's words in the introduction. And they wrote with the earnest intention of finding an appropriate, one might say a palatable, form for this knowledge, so that it would have the edifying, salutary, and occasionally even cathartic effects they wished it to have. Thus I think it is ultimately fair and proper, in spite of the evident difficulties raised by such an approach, to speak of the "art" of these early colonial writers. Art that reflects a faulty grasp of concepts and techniques, art that misses the mark in one way or another, is nonetheless recognizable—and, moreover, can be appreciated—as art. For all the technical and conceptual challenges that a particular text presents, we can still be witnesses to the *expressive* possibilities in the implied transaction between the writer and his putative readers, whether those readers were many or few.

In defending the truth-value of artistic expression, Hans-Georg Gadamer claims that "art is knowledge and the experience of the work of art is a sharing of this knowledge."[1] He is thinking here of art as a field distinct from science and other knowledge-producing disciplines, but it is worth considering the statement above as it applies to the work of writers like Smith, Bradford, Morton, and Williams. Such a consideration might well lead to an expanded version of Gadamer's claim: art is a kind of knowledge and also participates in other kinds of knowledge; the experience of the work of art is the sharing of not only this knowledge but also others. The element of artistic expression can be teased out and analyzed separately from the other sorts of knowledge for which it has been the vehicle, but the more productive approach is to think of these various forms of knowledge as existing in a dynamic dialectical relationship, a wider-ranging variation on the old familiar dance between form and content. We might conclude that the chains of our knowledge are forged from a complex alloy, containing significant measures of both art and science— and that to extend these chains from the past into the present is as much the office of the critic as it is of the historian.

In following out the logic of my metaphor, however, I am led to address a concern that encompasses but extends well beyond the issue of the reception of the knowledge shaped by several early Anglo-American writers. We might also be inclined to decide that the chains of knowledge only bind and burden us, that they obligate us to the past in ways that limit our freedom of movement in the present. Inevitably running parallel to the desire for more and better knowledge is the desire to lay such knowledge aside, to forget or defer it because it is too difficult, too foreign, too specialized, too tedious, too painful. More than censorship, incuriosity is a force capable of slowing and even halting the communication of knowledge. Every society has been incurious in one way or another at different stages of its evolution, but the desire *not* to know has lately come—again?—to seem a prominent American trait, one especially striking in a country overflowing with data, as ours now is. The growth of the "information economy" and of "knowledge work" has ironically been attended with the startling emergence of troubled quasi-colonial frontiers, including unexpected tracts of terra incognita in places that once seemed well known. Yet in the United States the pursuit and cultivation of knowledge about such places has been indifferent at best. Not only is there a general lack of interest in the characteristics of the other societies with which we must deal, but also an unusually high tolerance for institutional secrecy in regard to our political, military, and economic engagements with those societies. It is strange, if not fairly discouraging, to contemplate the possibility that the necessity and value of knowledge may have been felt more strongly in the trans-Atlantic commerce of the seventeenth century than in the global commerce of the twenty-first. My hope—which, quixotic as it may be, I believe I share with many people other than scholars—is that, in this still unfamiliar world dominated at so many levels by the United States of America, we as citizens will refuse to accept this state of affairs, that we will collectively reclaim a hunger, a passion, for knowing, and not (whether deliberately or negligently) break chains of knowledge that other scholars will have to reassemble painstakingly from a collection of fragmentary shapes in some distant, perhaps very different, future.

Appendix

—⚬—

Perry Miller on Roger Williams

Perry Miller was signally responsible for the mid-twentieth-century revival of critical interest in Roger Williams, and even half a century later students of Williams are likely to approach works such as *The Bloudy Tenent* with Miller leading the way. Yet in many respects Miller's commentary provides an unsatisfactory and even misleading introduction to Williams's thought. So eager is Miller to drive home the contrast between Williams and his orthodox opponents in Massachusetts that he vastly overstates not so much the content as the consequences of Williams's attachment to typology, and he glosses over equally significant factors in Williams's lengthy argument with John Cotton. In characterizing the typological method as the practice of a "rare and furtive brotherhood," Miller downplays the ubiquity of typology in Puritan thought, as Sacvan Bercovitch and Thomas Davis have demonstrated.[1] In further describing Williams's typology as involving "puzzles to be deciphered only in an imaginative realm outside history," as "black magic" and an "esoteric system," as composed of "fantastic windings" and "shifting hallucinations," and as "dangerously subjective," and "irresponsibly whimsical," if not "criminally insane," "a fever," a "mystagogic maze," "highly suspect," "bizarre," and "wild and impressionistic," Miller appears intent on stacking the deck with hyperbole in order to justify his thesis that Williams is a sort of theological wild man in comparison with his enemies.[2] At the same time, Miller quietly equates—if he is not confusing—typology with the most extravagant forms of allegorical interpretation.

Williams, however, seems much less interested in reinterpreting the Old Testament in abstractly spiritual terms than in pointing out that in prophetic terms the Old Testament is now an empty and useless artifact as far as the reformed church is concerned. This is to say that since the Old Testament has been fulfilled typologically in the New, it cannot be fulfilled in any other way or at any other time. Williams emphatically believes that biblical prophecies will one day become fact, but the only prophecies that matter—that are capable of fulfillment in historical time— are the prophecies in the New Testament, which are mainly found in the Book of Revelation.

His thinking on this point is manifest in many of his writings, but for brevity's sake I will illustrate it by way of one of a number of short tracts that Williams published in 1652, *The Hireling Ministry None of Christs*. He begins his argument with an exegesis of Revelation in order to show that the truly Christological order of apostolic ministry was interrupted by the great Apostasy (i.e., the rise of the Papacy) and will not be restored until the hour when Antichrist, the Pope, is defeated—an hour which, Williams observes, is probably coming soon but has certainly not yet arrived. Pending this event, all institutionally authorized and professionalized forms of ministry are fraudulent; the "first *Patterns* and Institutions of *Christ Jesus*" in the Gospels allow only for the "*Ministry* of *Prophets* or *Witnesses*," individuals from whatever walk of life who have been called by the Holy Spirit, the only "*true Sender*," to evangelize to the world (Williams identifies such individuals as "*Volunteers*"). The founders of the Bay Colony, however, have sidestepped these truths by speciously identifying their theocratic enterprise with Old Testament ordinances and, worse, with Old Testament "prophecy." This, Williams claims, is an utterly false position:

> The *Civil* state of the *Nations* being merely and essentially *civil*, cannot (Christianly) be called *Christian States*, after the pattern of that holy and typical Land of *Canaan*.
>
> . . . .
>
> [T]here is not a Title in the New *Testament* of *Christ Jesus*, that commits the *Forming* or *Reforming* of his *Spouse* and *Church* to the *civil* and *worldly* Powers.[3]

This is the nub of Williams's plea for the separation of church and state: after the coming of Christ, the old Israel lost its sacred status; the kingdom of the new dispensation is, in the words of John's gospel (18:36), "not of this world."[4] Any effort to conform it to the world—to combine the ecclesiastical with the civil—is thus a repudiation of Christ's *"Patterns and Institutions"* as revealed in the Gospels.

Here is where I believe that Miller's account of Williams's typology seizes the wrong end of the argument. Miller wants to present Williams as having abandoned, with the help of typological interpretation, the literal and historical sense of scripture in favor of a subjective and mystical vision of primitive Christianity. Williams does indeed celebrate the primitive church, but his argument centers on the idea that the New Testament tells us literally everything we need to know about such a church and the form that it should take in history. His typological reading of the Old Testament is primarily a means of reinforcing the absolute doctrinal primacy of the New Testament—a primacy that Williams claims the Bay colonists are always in danger of forgetting. Thus, typology is meaningful for Williams strictly between the covers of the Bible. The argument could even be advanced that Williams is engaging in a critique of a particular kind of typology that Bercovitch terms "historical,"[5] which in effect translates the Old Testament types into prophecies to be fulfilled in post-Resurrection time. Williams would understand such an approach as unbiblical and ultimately un-Christian, but one for which his opponents have a fatal weakness. Far from being (theologically, at least) heterodox and eccentric, Williams is a fundamentalist of a character that remains familiar today, whose convictions spring from an uncompromising sense of the unitary meaning of scripture; what sets him apart is his willingness, one might even say his compulsion, to press his convictions to the limit. As Anne Myles has said, "His distinctiveness appears in how stringently and consistently he applied his vision of the holy across a wide range of categories."[6] Williams is like his Puritan brethren, only more so—and therein lies the problem.

So why, given his extraordinary grasp of the intellectual controversies of seventeenth-century New England, did Miller opt for the particular distorting lens of "typology" through which to portray Williams? The answer may well turn on the rhetorical aspect of Miller's enterprise. In his essays on Williams, as throughout his work on New England, there is plenty of nuanced investigation of the shades and tints of Puritan thinking.

But Miller's "big picture" is invariably composed around bold ideological contrasts and knotty paradoxes that require agonistic resolutions. This dynamic sense of a world struggling cerebrally with itself continues to make Miller's work on Puritanism compelling despite the extensive and critical scrutiny it has received since his death in 1963. Where the contrasts and paradoxes are less obvious, however, he still wants to force them into lively operation. Miller's initial assertion about Williams is that those who treat him as a political figure are wrong, that he has to be understood in terms of his theology. Once Miller has made this claim, he must demonstrate that this theology sets Williams utterly apart from his plain-spoken contemporaries. Typology, as Miller defines it, then becomes the sign and seal of Williams's alienation. Yet there is little in Williams's use of typology that is exceptional or unorthodox; if anything, he applies it more responsibly than many of his peers. In this case, as perhaps in others, Miller appears to have sacrificed a degree of scholarly precision for the sake of intellectual drama.[7]

Notes

—ɯ—

Introduction

1. William Wood, *New England's Prospect*, 21, 25.

2. Wayne Franklin, *Discoverers, Explorers, Settlers: The Diligent Writers of Early America*, 7.

3. See, for instance, Mary Poovey, *A History of the Modern Fact: Problems of Knowledge in the Sciences of Wealth and Society*, xii–xiii, where Poovey employs the term as, presumably, a self-evident descriptor. It also appears in Jean Howard's introduction to *Marxist Shakespeares*, ed. Jean E. Howard and Scott Cutler Shershow, where she refers to Marxism as a "situated knowledge project" (6). When I asked her about the provenance of the term via e-mail, Howard replied that in her work the phrase has no specific lineage either, though it is at least partly inspired by her readings in feminist theory, especially where that theory criticizes or seeks to alter the conventions of Western epistemology. The knowledge projects I will be describing are not in the same register as Howard's, but I believe that in both cases the phrase points to what is at bottom a practical activity: the attempt to make (or remake) knowledge so that its content registers as different from the knowledge that existed previously.

4. I am not arguing that this assumption is either right or wrong; simply that it is common.

5. Frampton himself is a thoroughly obscure figure. He translated Marco Polo's *Travels* and a handful of other geographical works; otherwise little is known about his life. For overviews, see the respective entries for Dyer and Frampton in the *Dictionary of National Biography*. The only full-length study of Dyer is Ralph M. Sargent, *At the Court of Queen Elizabeth: The Life and Lyrics of Sir Edward Dyer*, which collects many details about Dyer's activities from his surviving correspondence. Sargent quotes the dedication to Dyer from Frampton's 1579 translation of Polo, which is quite similar to the one in *Joyfull Newes;* Dyer is a "special Gentleman, a lover of knowledge"; there is "no man" to whom "so many Scholars" and "so many travelers" are "bound" (56–57).

6. John Frampton, *Joyfull Newes Out of the New Founde Worlde, Written in Spanish by Nicholas Monardes Physician of Seville and Englished by John Frampton, Merchant*

Anno 1577, 4. Stephen Gaselee's introduction (1:vi–vii) indicates that Frampton's translation derives from Monardes's collection of the different parts of his treatise into a single volume, entitled *Primera y segunda y tercera partes de la historia medicinal de las cosas que se traen de nuestras Indias Occidentales que sirven en Medicina* (Seville, 1574). Monardes (1493–1588) apparently spent most of his long life and medical career in Seville, occasionally writing on other botanical topics (viii–ix). Like Columbus's chronicler Peter Martyr and a number of other European writers on the New World, he did not feel the need actually to go there.

7. Andrew Barnaby and Lisa J. Schnell, *Literate Experience: The Work of Knowing in Seventeenth-Century English Writing,* 2; Andrew Fitzmaurice, *Humanism and America: An Intellectual History of English Colonisation, 1500–1625,* 102. Fitzmaurice offers a useful discussion of the influence of humanist conceptions of rhetoric on colonialist promotional literature in seventeenth-century England (102–29).

8. These pressures even extend, Peter Charles Hoffer has argued, to the operations of the five senses; see his *Sensory Worlds in Early America.*

9. Compare this passage from the essay "Des coches":

> Our world has just discovered another one: and who will answer for its being the last of its brothers, since up till now its existence was unknown to the daemons, to the Sybils, and to ourselves? It is no less big and full and solid than our own; its limbs are as well developed: yet it is so new, such a child, that we are still teaching it its ABC; a mere fifty years ago it knew nothing of writing, weights, and measures, clothing, any sort of corn or vine. It was still naked at the breast, living only by what its nursing Mother provided. If we are right to conclude that our end is nigh, and that poet is right that his world is young, then that other world will only be emerging into light when ours is leaving it. (Michel de Montaigne, *The Essays: A Selection,* 342)

10. Edmundo O'Gorman, *The Invention of America: An Inquiry into the Historical Nature of the New World and the Meaning of Its History,* 134; J. H. Elliott, *The Old World and the New, 1492–1650,* 15.

11. Claude Lévi-Strauss, *The Savage Mind,* 17, 19, 22.

12. See, for example, Tzvetan Todorov, *The Conquest of America: The Question of the Other,* 98–123, and Stephen Greenblatt, *Renaissance Self-Fashioning: From More to Shakespeare,* 222–54.

13. Franklin, *Discoverers,* 6.

14. For a nice illustration of what is assumed under the concept of a discursive field, see Peter Hulme's definition of "colonial discourse":

> an ensemble of linguistically-based practices unified by their common deployment in the management of colonial relationships . . . sets of questions and assumptions, methods of procedure and analysis, and kinds of writing and imagery, normally separated out into the discrete areas of military

strategy, political order, social reform, imaginative literature, personal memoir and so on. (Peter Hulme, *Colonial Encounters: Europe and the Native Caribbean, 1492–1797*, 2)

15. Strictly speaking there is just a single edition of the *Generall Historie*, but it was issued from the same plates seven times between 1624 and 1632, with slightly different title pages. The number of issues in a relatively short period suggests that Smith's book experienced some degree of popularity. See the bibliographical note to the text in Philip L. Barbour, ed., *The Complete Works of Captain John Smith, 1580–1631*, 2:487–88.

16. For a short summary of the manuscript's history, see Douglas Anderson, *William Bradford's Books: "Of Plimmoth Plantation" and the Printed Word*, 1–2.

17. Hayden White, "The Value of Narrativity in the Representation of Reality," 9. Thomas Scanlan has associated a notion of allegory with colonial texts in *Colonial Writing and the New World, 1583–1671: Allegories of Desire;* see esp. 9–19.

18. John J. Teunissen and Evelyn J. Hinz, eds., *A Key into the Language of America*, 90.

19. The dilemma for the critic of the textual past of early Anglo-America is well illustrated in Ivy Schweitzer, *The Work of Self-Representation: Lyric Poetry in Colonial New England*. Schweitzer offers a thought-provoking feminist reading of the "New England mind," but only one of the four authors she discusses, the inevitable Anne Bradstreet, is female.

20. J. H. Elliott, "Final Reflections: The Old World and the New Revisited," 399.

1. The Incoherent Colonist: Troubled Knowledge in John Smith's *Generall Historie of Virginia*

1. Barbour, *Complete Works*, 3:300–301, 288, 286.

2. Myra Jehlen, "History before the Fact; or, Captain John Smith's Unfinished Symphony," 680–81.

3. This is something of a favorite passage for critics of colonial texts; see, for instance, Jeffrey Knapp, *An Empire Nowhere: England, America, and Literature from "Utopia" to "The Tempest,"* 2.

4. Jehlen, "History before the Fact," 687, 688, 689, 690, 692.

5. Peter Hulme, "Making No Bones: A Response to Myra Jehlen," 185; Myra Jehlen, "A Response to Peter Hulme," 191.

6. Hulme, *Colonial Encounters*, 139. Hulme is contrasting Virginia with New England, where "coherence was largely provided by the ideology of Puritanism" (139). For "innermost propulsion," see Perry Miller, *Errand into the Wilderness*, viii.

7. My source for the *Generall Historie* is volume 2 of Barbour, *Complete Works*.

The best modern account of Jamestown's decline and fall remains Wesley Frank Craven, *Dissolution of the Virginia Company: The Failure of a Colonial Experiment*. For a longer-term view, see Edmund S. Morgan, *American Slavery, American Freedom: The Ordeal of Colonial Virginia*.

8. Franklin, *Discoverers*, 187, 191. I would qualify my agreement with the last quotation by saying that, in Smith's case at least, the primary voice never manages to exclude the other voices struggling to speak, nor does it ever fully control the "center"; see my discussion of the Algonquian "map" and the bag of gunpowder, below.

9. In addition to Hulme's chapter on Smith and Pocahontas in *Colonial Encounters* (137–73), see Mary C. Fuller's discussion in *Voyages in Print: English Travel to America, 1576–1624*, 103–40.

10. The most incongruous feature of the list is the insertion of "*Wepenter*, A cookold" between "*Shacquohocan*, A stone" and "*Suckahanna*, Water." Knapp, reading the list in *A Map of Virginia*, also notes this peculiarity but treats it, curiously, as a joke on Smith's part (*Empire Nowhere*, 209). Knapp is hewing to his thesis that "trifling" is a central element of both colonial activity and that activity's literary representations, but the interpretation here seems unduly elaborate, since there are no obvious indications in the way Smith presents the list that he is being either frivolous or ironic—and subtle humor is not notably one of the arrows in Smith's rhetorical quiver.

11. Barbour, *Complete Works*, 2:130, 131–32. Knapp, *Empire Nowhere*, 209, quotes the second excerpt in his discussion of the word list from *A Map of Virginia*. The passage also makes an appearance in Bruce R. Smith, "Mouthpieces: Native American Voices in Thomas Harriot's *A True and Brief Report of . . . Virginia* [*sic*], Gaspar Pérez de Villagrá's *Historia de la Nuevo México*, and Captain John Smith's *General History of Virginia*," 514, where the argument is that "these reported speeches serve as a defense against the Indians' frightening otherness" (514), in the sense that John Smith denatures the character of Native American speech by transforming it into writing.

12. The same phenomenon occurs in Williams's *A Key into the Language of America*, though almost certainly its causes are different there (see my Chapter 4). A number of recent studies have combined readings of English historical documents with the available anthropological and archaeological data so as to provide fuller accounts of an indigenous social and political system that Smith and his cohorts understood only very partially, and to describe more precisely the complex cultural transaction between the representatives of that system and the Europeans who were intruding upon it. See, for example, Karen Ordahl Kupperman, *Indians and English: Facing Off in Early America*, Margaret Holmes Williamson, *Powhatan Lords of Life and Death: Command and Consent in Seventeenth-Century Virginia*, and William Boelhower, "Mapping the Gift Path: Exchange and Rivalry in John Smith's 'A True Relation.'"

13. Barbour, *Complete Works*, 2:175–76.

14. Ibid., 2:147. The shift from first person to third person occurs frequently in the *Generall Historie;* it may or may not imply the presence of an author, or authors, other than Smith. Given the (still) confused—and confusing—state of the text, perhaps the firmest ground to stand on here is to regard Smith as an extremely "active" editor, always shaping the material at his disposal to suit his own ends, and imposing his own personality on the work of others. Richard Hakluyt the Younger's *Principall Navigations Voiages and Discoveries of the English Nation* (1st ed., 1589; 2d ed., 1598–1600) would have provided a powerful model for Smith's work in this respect.

15. Barbour, *Complete Works*, 2:156. Fuller alludes to both the episode of the blue beads and that of the compass, describing the compass as

> an attractive artifact, about which he [Smith] can say what he wishes. The artifact is mystified as an object rather than explicated as a device; it in this way like other English cultural goods of less practical value, like the blue beads Smith successfully offers Powhatan on a later occasion. (*Voyages in Print*, 96–97)

In either case, Fuller emphasizes the mystification rather than the mystery inherent in the transaction. I would argue that rather than being mere means to an end, both the compass dial and the beads are cryptic emblems of Smith's omniscience—or at least that is what he intends them to be. For yet another account of the ambiguities surrounding the compass episode, see Steven Mullaney, "Imaginary Conquests: European Material Technologies and the Colonial Mirror Stage," 21–22.

16. Barbour, *Complete Works*, 2:147. As Kupperman points out, the whole exchange would have been almost completely nonverbal, since neither party understood much of the language of the other. This may help to account for the transitory effect of Smith's description of the world. See Karen Ordahl Kupperman, ed., *Captain John Smith: A Select Edition of His Writings*, 60n12.

17. Barbour, *Complete Works*, 2:150.

18. Ibid., 2:150.

19. Ibid., 2:195.

20. Ibid., 2:195, 196. In book 3, chapter 10, the chieftain Okaning expresses similar sentiments to Smith rather more bluntly: "We perceive and well know you intend to destroy us" (ibid., 2:208).

21. Smith, "Mouthpieces," 510, 511, 513, 514. What is most problematic for me about the argument of this essay is the apparent claim that any effort by a colonial author to render Native American speech in written form is invalid and produces merely "the *illusion* of knowledge" (515; emphasis in original). This seems to me to lead close to an infinite regress: since the sound-world of indige-

nous culture is all-important, and since duplicating it on the page is impossible, then almost all writing about Native Americans as speakers in the historical past basically becomes nonsense; in effect, Powhatan would be permanently silenced as an articulate being. I cannot imagine that this is the effect that Bruce Smith intends to achieve in his own writing, but his thesis would make such a consequence very difficult to avoid.

22. Barbour, *Complete Works,* 2:196.

23. Ibid., 2:261.

24. Ibid.

25. This essay has appeared in many versions in many places, most prominently in Stephen Greenblatt, *Shakespearean Negotiations: The Circulation of Social Energy in Renaissance England,* 21–65. My quotations are from this source.

26. Ibid., 36.

27. Ibid., 36, 37.

28. Smith returned to England in 1609 after being seriously burned when a bag of gunpowder exploded as he slept in his pinnace on a downriver trip to Jamestown; at the time he was already under threat of removal from the presidency, a victim of the weak economic condition of the colony, of his own high-handed approach to governing Jamestown, and of a fair share of personal ill will toward him. See Barbour, *Complete Works,* 1:268–75.

29. Fitzmaurice, *Humanism and America,* 137.

30. E. G. R. Taylor, ed., *The Original Writings and Correspondence of the Two Richard Hakluyts,* 2:274, 275, 280. Fitzmaurice, *Humanism and America,* 177–86, argues for a Machiavellian strand in Smith's writing and thinking, reflected in Smith's frequent presentation of himself as acting decisively and without regard for protocol in the face of duplicity on the part of both Powhatan and the colonists.

31. Sir Walter Ralegh, *The Discoverie of the Large, Rich and Bewtiful Empyre of Guiana,* 75.

32. See Gary B. Nash, "The Image of the Indian in the Southern Colonial Mind," and Richard R. Johnson, "The Search for a Usable Indian: An Aspect of the Defense of Colonial New England."

33. D. W. Meinig, *The Shaping of America: A Geographical Perspective on 500 Years of History,* 1:65–66, 71–72.

34. Michael Warner, "What's Colonial about Colonial America?" 57, 58.

35. This term is indeed becoming more frequent in colonial studies. See, for instance, Kathleen Donegan, "'As Dying, yet Behold We Live': Catastrophe and Interiority in Bradford's *Of Plymouth Plantation.*" Donegan refers to "the literature of settlement as a literature of unsettlement, a history of colonial aporia" (15).

36. Barbour, *Complete Works,* 2:298–99; Kupperman, *Captain John Smith,* 12. One of the fascinating features of the *Generall Historie* is its "synchronic" character:

Smith has made little effort to create or organize any sense of historical development in his own thinking, so that we have a difficult time as readers in distin-
guishing between "earlier" and "later" perspectives; they all seem to occupy the
same moment in the textual "present." In this sense, Smith's book is one of the
least historical of histories.

37. Barbour, *Complete Works*, 2:298.

38. See Hayden White, *Metahistory: The Historical Imagination in Nineteenth-
Century Europe*, esp. 230–64.

39. The notion of historical interpretation as a process of rethinking past
thoughts comes from R. G. Collingwood's *The Idea of History;* see the following
passage, for instance:

> When a man thinks historically, he has before him certain documents or
> relics of the past. His business is to discover what the past was which has
> left these relics behind it. For example, the relics are certain written words;
> and in that case he has to discover what the person who wrote those words
> meant by them. This means discovering the thought (in the widest sense of
> that word . . .) which he expressed by them. To discover what this thought
> was, the historian must think it again for himself. (282–83)

40. In *Truth and Method,* his magisterial defense of hermeneutics, Hans-Georg
Gadamer offers a decidedly optimistic view of the problem of historical distance,
suggesting that what he refers to as "effective-historical consciousness"—the consciousness of one's own localized position in relation to the past—is the beginning of inventive critical activity:

> the important thing is to recognize the distance in time as a positive and
> productive possibility of understanding. It is not a yawning abyss, but is
> filled with the continuity of custom and tradition, in the light of which all
> that is handed down presents itself to us. Here it is not too much to speak of
> a genuine productivity of process. (*Truth and Method,* 264–65)

Gadamer's point, as I take it, is that the difficulty of understanding the past is a
given; since we cannot stand outside of history in order to grasp its significance—since, in Gadamer's own formulation, "history does not belong to us, but
we belong to it" (ibid., 245)—we come to recognize that a proper study of the
past means puzzling out, perhaps not always with ideal success, the various ways
that history encloses us without its ever becoming perfectly, immediately available to us. It is out of the same recognition—a consciousness of our perennial desire to know where we as human beings stand in time—that we read old texts and
try to make sense of them long after they were written.

2. Silent Partners: Historical Representation in
William Bradford's *Of Plymouth Plantation*

1. Robert Daly, "William Bradford's Vision of History," 557. This memorable sentence also provides the point of departure for Mark L. Sargent's essay on Bradford, "William Bradford's 'Dialogue' with History," 390.

2. David Levin, "William Bradford: The Value of Puritan Historiography"; Alan B. Howard, "Art and History in Bradford's *Of Plymouth Plantation*"; Walter P. Wenska, "Bradford's Two Histories: Pattern and Paradigm in *Of Plymouth Plantation*"; Franklin, *Discoverers*, 165–78; Sargent, "Bradford's 'Dialogue,'" 408. Howard, "Art and History," 237–42, offers a pungent historical summary of the standard views on Bradford; in "Bradford's Two Histories," Wenska, within a broadly providentialist reading filtered (dubiously) through Eriksonian psychology, makes the very sensible point that the two parts of the history were written at widely separated intervals and thus reflect different levels of Bradford's experience with the fortunes of the colony.

3. William Haller, *The Rise of Puritanism; or, The Way to the New Jerusalem as Set Forth in Pulpit and Press from Thomas Cartwright to John Lilburne and John Milton, 1570–1643*, 190. The bon mot is the work of Peter Weed. For a definition of providential history, I look no farther than the one provided by Francis Bacon in book 2 of *The Advancement of Learning* (1605):

> History of Providence . . . containeth that excellent correspondence which is between God's revealed will and his secret will; which though it be so obscure as for the most part it is not legible to the natural man; no, nor many times to those that behold it from the tabernacle; yet at some times it pleaseth God, for our better establishment and the confuting of those which are as without God in the world, to write it in such text and capital letters that, as the prophet saith, "he that runneth by may read it." (Brian Vickers, ed., *Francis Bacon*, 185)

4. John Griffith, "*Of Plymouth Plantation* as a Mercantile Epic," 235; Kenneth Alan Hovey, "The Theology of History in *Of Plymouth Plantation* and Its Predecessors," 64, 61. For a recent, economically oriented reading of Bradford, see Michelle Burnham, "Merchants, Money, and the Economics of 'Plain Style' in William Bradford's *Of Plymouth Plantation*."

5. Jesper Rosenmeier, "'With My Owne Eyes': William Bradford's *Of Plymouth Plantation*," 98.

6. For a specific application of "body criticism" to Bradford, see Donegan, "'As Dying, yet Behold We Live,'" in which Donegan argues that *Of Plymouth Plantation* constructs colonial identity around the trope of an injured, alienated body situated uncertainly between life and death.

7. Samuel Eliot Morison, ed., *Of Plymouth Plantation, 1620–1647, by William*

Bradford Sometime Governor Thereof, 9, 8, 19, 46. I have used Morison's edition as my primary working text but have also occasionally consulted the 1898 Commonwealth of Massachusetts edition, *Bradford's History "Of Plimoth Plantation,"* and the 1912 Massachusetts Historical Society edition, *History of Plymouth Plantation.*

8. See Hayden White, "The Historical Text as Literary Artifact," which offers a nicely compressed presentation of White's ideas on this topic.

9. The concluding verse of Judges is as follows: "In those days there was no king in Israel; every man did that which was right in his own eyes" (Judges 21:25).

10. Morison, *Of Plymouth Plantation,* 13.

11. Ibid., 58, 61–63. On Cape Cod as wilderness, see David Laurence, "William Bradford's American Sublime."

12. Morison, *Of Plymouth Plantation,* 61–62, 72.

13. Anderson, *Bradford's Books,* 177. For Johnson's text, see J. Franklin Jameson, ed., *Johnson's Wonder-Working Providence, 1628–1651.*

14. See Anderson, *Bradford's Books,* 32–46, and F. J. Levy, *Tudor Historical Thought,* 167–201.

15. These are, not surprisingly, also the central topoi of epic poetry. On the links between the epic genre and colonial activity, see David Quint, *Epic and Empire: Politics and Generic Form from Virgil to Milton.* On history as *res gestae,* see Arthur B. Ferguson, *Clio Unbound: Perception of the Social and Cultural Past in Renaissance England,* 3–27.

16. Emory Elliott, *New England Puritan Literature,* 215, 216–17.

17. Vickers, *Francis Bacon,* 175, 177, 183.

18. Anderson, *Bradford's Books,* 141–45, offers a useful discussion of this shift, describing Morton as "an agent of cultural and historical acceleration who is quickly helping to erode the distinction between 'old' and 'new' worlds, creating the technological conditions by which the nexus of war and traffic . . . might establish itself firmly in New England" (144). For a comparison of Bradford's and Morton's narratives, see Thomas Cartelli, "Transplanting Disorder: The Construction of Misrule in Morton's *New English Canaan* and Bradford's *Of Plymouth Plantation.*"

19. Morison, *Of Plymouth Plantation,* 204, 203. William Cronon uses Bradford's comment about the change in Native American affairs to illustrate the point that "wampum was part of the reorganization of Indian economic and political life in the wake of the epidemics: competition for its acquisition established new leaders, promoted dependence on European traders, and helped shift the tribute obligations which had previously existed among Indian villages" (*Changes in the Land: Indians, Colonists, and the Ecology of New England,* 97).

20. Morison, *Of Plymouth Plantation,* 203.

21. Ibid., 10.

22. Ibid., 16. The information on the Netherlands is drawn from Henry Martin

Dexter and Morton Dexter, *The England and Holland of the Pilgrims*, 413–14, 497. The satirical quotation appears in this same volume on 419, though its original source is the anonymous text *The Dutch Drawn to the Life* (London, 1664), 48.

23. Michael Kammen, *Colonial New York: A History*, 37, 61–62 (comment by Jogues on 61), 58–60. The proliferation of languages was the result of the West India Company's strategy of recruiting colonists from other parts of Europe, since Dutch citizens, enjoying considerable prosperity at home, were reluctant to immigrate to New Netherland. See Kammen, *Colonial New York*, 36–38. The colony lasted for forty years, from the arrival of the first civilians in 1624 until it was ceded to the Duke of York in 1664, and was underpopulated and undercapitalized during most of that period, largely due to the parsimony of the Dutch West India Company.

24. Morison, *Of Plymouth Plantation*, 378–80.

25. Quoted in Kammen, *Colonial New York*, 37. New Netherland, as many historians have noted, displays interesting parallels with the Virginia colony during its first fifty years. The Pilgrims' relations with the Virginians were marked by a similar sort of ambivalence. See, for instance, Bradford's account of the stranded Virginia-bound traveler Mr. Fells (Morison, *Of Plymouth Plantation*, 191–92). Concerns about the Virginia enterprise (most of them probably justified) surface early on in the Pilgrims' transactions; see Robert Cushman's letter of May 8, 1619 (Morison, *Of Plymouth Plantation*, 355–57).

26. Morison, *Of Plymouth Plantation*, 25. Bruce McLeod, in *The Geography of Empire in English Literature, 1580–1745*, 107–15, interestingly stresses Bradford's concern with the deployment of *space* in and around Plymouth. However, McLeod's argument follows the trend of so many other dualistic readings of Bradford in treating him as being on the inside looking out at what McLeod calls "the dynamism of capital accumulation" (111–12); hence he gives little attention to the "tedious notes about the colonies' business affairs" (109). I am arguing that the "dynamism" McLeod speaks of is from the outset as much inside Plymouth as it is outside of it.

27. Morison, *Of Plymouth Plantation*, 204.

28. Ibid., 204.

29. Ibid., 204–5.

30. Ibid., 205.

31. Ibid., 76, 208, 205–6. In spite of their claim to form a new body politic, the founders of Plymouth acknowledge themselves to be "loyal subjects of our dread Sovereign Lord King James." The representatives of Plymouth later threaten Morton with a "penalty" that will be "more than he could bear—His Majesty's displeasure" (ibid., 75, 209).

32. Ibid., 206–7.

33. Ibid., 207 (emphasis mine).

34. W. H. Walsh, *Philosophy of History: An Introduction*, 24–25; see also 59–63.

35. Morison, *Of Plymouth Plantation*, 210. For "two-eyedness," see A. P. Rossiter, *Angel with Horns and Other Shakespeare Lectures*, 62; also 51, 292.

36. Morison, *Of Plymouth Plantation*, 207.

37. See, for instance, ibid., 239. Anderson, *Bradford's Books*, 148, comments on the frequent use of proverbial matter in Bradford's treatment of Allerton, suggesting that this is Bradford's way of counterbalancing the often confusing discussion of Allerton's commercial activities.

38. Morison, *Of Plymouth Plantation*, 211, 216. Allerton and Morton appear to be linked to one another in Bradford's thinking: the detailed examination of Allerton's actions begins immediately after Bradford closes his discussion of the "battle" at Ma-re Mount (210).

39. Ibid., 218; Bradford, *History of Plymouth Plantation*, 1:451n.

40. Morison, *Of Plymouth Plantation*, 86. In his article on Allerton in the *Dictionary of American Biography*, R. G. Usher calls him "third in importance during the first ten years at Plymouth" and notes that he was the only officer of the colony other than Bradford from 1621 to 1624. After his disgrace at Plymouth he eventually settled in New Haven, where he built up a trade on "his own particular" with New Netherland, Virginia, and English interests in the Caribbean.

41. Morison, *Of Plymouth Plantation*, 233–34. The idea of Allerton being "in the middle" takes a sinister turn in Bradford's description of the controversy over whether Plymouth should cooperate with the London partners in supporting Edward Ashley's dubious fur-trading venture at Penobscot: "they [at Plymouth] considered that if they joined not in the business, they knew Mr. Allerton would be with them [the London partners] in it, and so would swim as it were between both to the prejudice of both, but of themselves [at Plymouth] especially" (ibid., 220).

42. Ibid., 241–42, 244, 245, 256.

43. Ibid., 221.

44. Bradford continues the story in the annal for 1630; the ship in question—apparently the *Friendship*—encountered bad weather and returned to port, failing to reach New England that year (ibid., 226–27).

45. Richard Helgerson, *Forms of Nationhood: The Elizabethan Writing of England*, 163–91.

3. Importing the Metropolis: The Poetics of Urbanity in Thomas Morton's *New English Canaan*

1. Cartelli, "Transplanting Disorder," 279; John Seelye, *Prophetic Waters: The River in Early American Life and Literature*, 169; Daniel Shea, "'Our Professed Old Adversary': Thomas Morton and the Naming of New England," 53.

2. Charles Francis Adams Jr., ed., *New English Canaan of Thomas Morton*, 80, 96. Shea, "'Adversary,'" provides an interesting note on the Adams family's propri-

etary connection with Mount Wollaston (67–68n7). I use the Adams edition as my working text. I have also referred regularly to the edition of Jack Dempsey, *New English Canaan by Thomas Morton of "Merrymount": Text, Notes, Biography, and Criticism.* While it is good to have a reasonably priced paperback version of the text readily available, this edition, a digital reproduction of a dissertation, is eccentric in many respects, including in its editorial practices, and should be used with caution. It has appeared in several variants, the earliest of which contains two parts under one cover, paginated and indexed separately, reflecting the original division of Dempsey's dissertation into separate volumes. Therefore my citations to Dempsey refer to both part and page. A subsequent printing (also 2000) includes only the first part; this is also available in portable document format (2001). The material at 2:83–125 has appeared in essay form in Jack Dempsey, "Reading the Revels: The Riddle of May Day in *New English Canaan*."

3. See Morison, *Of Plymouth Plantation*, 204–10. I have discussed Bradford's view of Morton in the previous chapter.

4. Ibid., 62.

5. Adams, *New English Canaan*, 121.

6. I am mindful here of a debt to Jacob Burckhardt's seminal notion of "the State as the outcome of reflection and calculation, the State as a work of art" (*The Civilization of the Renaissance in Italy*, 4), though in my own account of institutional style I would put less emphasis on "reflection and calculation," since style appears to me always to involve a fortuitous combination of intentions and contingencies; in other words, it is only partly a matter of (and for) aesthetics.

7. John Winthrop, *Winthrop Papers*, 2:295. On the initial development of Shawmut, see Darrett B. Rutman, *Winthrop's Boston: Portrait of a Puritan Town, 1630–1649*, 23–40. The pattern of settlement in the early years tended to skirt the hills and became densest around Great Cove, the area that became Boston Harbor.

8. On the location of Ma-re Mount, see Adams, *New English Canaan*, 9–12, or the revised version of the same material in Charles Francis Adams Jr., *Three Episodes of Massachusetts History*, 1:166–68. In *New England's Crises and Cultural Memory: Literature, Politics, History, Religion, 1620–1860*, 55, John McWilliams quotes the same passage from *Three Episodes* that heads my chapter, while suggesting that Adams's later book presents a revised, more tolerant view of Morton than prevailed in his edition of *New English Canaan*, the result perhaps of Adams's own experience of failure on the frontier as president of the Union Pacific Railroad during its slide into bankruptcy in the late 1880s (53–55).

9. Adams, *New English Canaan*, 115, 179, 180, 114, 111, 109. The fullest versions of the pastoralist argument are probably found in Donald F. Connors, *Thomas Morton*, 72–80, and Robert D. Arner, "Pastoral Celebration and Satire in Thomas Morton's *New English Canaan*." Arner's essay is strongly influenced by C. L. Bar-

ber's landmark *Shakespeare's Festive Comedy: A Study of Dramatic Form and Its Relation to Social Custom.* See also Seelye, *Prophetic Waters,* 170–80. Dempsey, *New English Canaan,* describes Morton as a "pastoral realist" (2:151n2; see also 1:xxxii).

10. Adams, *New English Canaan,* 114.

11. Ibid., 114. Quoting this same passage, Cartelli points out that "The representation of the New World as a virgin awaiting insemination and cultivation by resourceful and energetic Europeans is a conceit that by this time [Morton's time] had already become an iconographic cliché" ("Transplanting Disorder," 258). A notorious earlier example is the passage at the end of Ralegh's *Discoverie of Guiana,* in which Guiana "hath yet her maidenhead, never sacked, turned, nor wrought" (73); see also Donne's "Elegy 2: To His Mistress Going to Bed," lines 27–30, where the narrator compares his lovemaking to colonization: "O my America, my new found land, / My kingdom, safeliest when with one man manned, / My mine of precious stones, my empery, / How blessed am I in this discovering thee" (John Carey, ed., *John Donne: A Critical Edition of the Major Works,* 13). Dempsey calls attention to this passage in his biography of Morton in *New English Canaan,* 2:50.

12. Adams, *New English Canaan,* 122.

13. Wolfgang Stechow, *Dutch Landscape Painting in the Seventeenth Century,* 7–8.

14. See Adams, *New English Canaan,* 139, 141, 172, 184, 217. Other references to Wood occur at 154–55, 238.

15. Wood, *New England's Prospect,* 15, 75.

16. Ibid., 17, 88.

17. Seelye, *Prophetic Waters,* 155.

18. Wood, *New England's Prospect,* 57–58, 59.

19. Adams, *New English Canaan,* 110.

20. David Riggs lists among Jonson's Inn acquaintances Thomas Overbury, John Beaumont, Francis Bacon, Sir John Harington, John Donne, John Selden, and Francis Beaumont (*Ben Jonson: A Life,* 56). The overall historical record of the Inns of Court is exceptionally and frustratingly sparse. This is even more the case with the Inns of Chancery, in which students mainly learned to produce writs and other legal documents before (perhaps) moving on to more advanced legal study. The Inns of Chancery have all disappeared; Clifford's Inn was the last, dissolving in 1903, its main building demolished. Only its gatehouse survives, a little off Fleet Street. None of the inns has ever incorporated, and their systems of governance are customary rather than formal. As a result, their record keeping has been extremely erratic over many centuries, and there are many periods for which little or no information exists about their operation. In the best available study of the inns in the sixteenth and seventeenth centuries, Wilfrid R. Prest begins by saying that they "still occupy an historical no-man's land" (*The Inns of Court under Elizabeth I and the Early Stuarts, 1590–1640,* vii). For a useful short introduction to Clifford's Inn, see Clare Rider, "Lost in the Past: The Rediscovered

Archives of Clifford's Inn." In his biography of Morton, Dempsey devotes a chapter, much of it speculative, to Morton's career at Clifford's Inn (Dempsey, *New
English Canaan*, 2:41–61). Though this account does not overcome the problems
caused by the nearly complete absence of facts about Morton's early life, it does
offer an interesting description of the general ambience of the inns in the 1590s.

21. Adams, *New English Canaan*, 214. On the relationship of Morton's book to
the Jonsonian masque, see Shea, "'Adversary,'" 56–61. Arner, "Pastoral Celebration," briefly notes the possible influence of *The Alchemist* on Morton's treatment
of the Massachusetts separatists (228n22).

22. See C. H. Herford and Percy Simpson, eds., *Ben Jonson*, 8:46. Neither
Adams nor Dempsey makes the connection to Jonson's character. It is just possible that this name represents an obscure jibe at William Wood, once again.

23. Adams, *New English Canaan*, 290; Herford and Simpson, *Ben Jonson*, 8:84.

24. Adams, *New English Canaan*, 291, 294–95. Morton has already identified
himself with the Hydra in chapter 15. On the possible circulation of the poem in
London, see Morton's introduction to the "Baccanal Triumphe" at the beginning
of chapter 17, and Adams's note on the passage in *New English Canaan*, 290.

25. Ibid., 291n; Herford and Simpson, *Ben Jonson*, 1:63, 2:339, 341.

26. Andrew McRae, "'On the Famous Voyage': Ben Jonson and Civic Space."
For another thoughtful recent reading of the poem, see Bruce Boehrer,
"Horatian Satire in Jonson's 'On the Famous Voyage,'" 9–26. Boehrer argues per-
suasively for Jonson's debt to Horace's Satire 1.5, usually called "A Journey to
Brundisium." It might be overvaluing Morton's classical learning to say that in
imitating "On the Famous Voyage" he would have had any sense of Horace as an
underlying poetic model—though there is at least the possibility that the con-
cluding Latin tag in *New English Canaan*, "*Cynthius aurem vellet,*" is borrowed from
Horace's Satire 1.9 rather than Virgil's *Eclogues*. See Dempsey, *New English
Canaan*, 1:199.

27. Herford and Simpson, *Ben Jonson*, 8:85, 87, 88, 89.

28. Adams, *New English Canaan*, 293, 291n, 294. Adams comments dryly in his
notes, "'Brave Christmas gambols' were, it may be remarked, not greatly in
vogue in the Plymouth of 1628" (294).

29. See ibid., 279, where Morton refers to the May Day activities as "Revels."

30. Ibid., 254; see 252–55 for Morton's complete account of the event. As
Adams points out in his note to this passage, *wotawquenauge* (not *wotawquenange*,
which appears to be either Morton's or a typesetter's mistake) actually means
"coat-men," a term that also appears in Williams's *Key into the Language*. The correct term would be *chauquaqock*, "knife-men." Kupperman, in "Thomas Morton,
Historian," argues that Morton's version of the Wessagusset massacre is much
more accurate and incisive than the accounts, such as Edward Winslow's, that
emerged from Plymouth.

31. See Adams, *New English Canaan*, 332; Morton also describes the ordeal of
"Innocence Faircloth" (Philip Ratcliff), accused by "Captain Littleworth" (John

Endicott) of blasphemy against the Salem church, and sentenced to "have his tongue bored through; his nose slit; his face branded; his ears cut; his body to be whip'd in ever several plantation of their Jurisdiction; and a fine of forty pounds impos'd, with perpetual banishment." According to Morton, Sir Christopher Gardiner was able to *mitigate* the sentence to whipping, ear docking, fining, confiscation of goods, and banishment (ibid., 319–20).

32. Ibid., 339; see also 334: "If this be one of their gifts, then Machevill had as good gifts as they." In the third book (338–42), Morton recounts the Pilgrims' efforts to rid themselves of Gardiner, prompting Gardiner later to write a sonnet about "Wolfs in Sheeps clothing" (341).

33. Ibid., 320.

34. McRae, "'On the Famous Voyage,'" 25, 30.

35. For the poems, see Adams, *New English Canaan*, 266, 275, 277–78, 279–80, 315.

36. Michael Zuckerman, "Pilgrims in the Wilderness: Community, Modernity, and the Maypole at Merry Mount," 276; Cartelli, "Transplanting Disorder," 280.

37. Matt Cohen, "Morton's Maypole and the Indians: Publishing in Early New England," 6, 13.

38. Adams, *New English Canaan*, 176.

39. In his fascinating social history of colonial taverns, David W. Conroy points out that by the 1670s these venues were frequently employed to hold court sessions and various kinds of municipal meetings, in spite of Puritan concerns about alcohol consumption and other incitements to civil disorder. See Conroy, *In Public Houses: Drink and the Revolution of Authority in Colonial Massachusetts*, 12–56.

40. Adams, *New English Canaan*, 279–80.

41. Ibid., 342–43, 344.

4. American Consciences:
Roger Williams's Field of Inquiry

With the exception of *Key into the Language*, for which I use the Teunissen and Hinz edition, all selections from Williams's works are taken from the 1963 Russell and Russell edition of *The Complete Writings of Roger Williams* (hereinafter referred to as *Complete Writings*). The first six volumes of this edition reproduce the earlier "complete" edition of the Narragansett Club (Providence, 1866); the seventh volume, edited by Perry Miller, consists of previously uncollected texts and Miller's short but important monograph "Roger Williams: An Essay in Interpretation."

1. A recent exception is Scott L. Pratt, *Native Pragmatism: Rethinking the Roots of American Philosophy*, 78–119. Pratt makes the intriguing if not wholly convincing argument that Williams's theory of religious toleration was modeled on his experiences among the Narragansetts.

2. John Garrett, *Roger Williams: Witness beyond Christendom, 1603–1683*, 122.

3. Patricia E. Rubertone, *Grave Undertakings: An Archaeology of Roger Williams and the Narragansett Indians*, 3.

4. See Joseph J. Ellis, *American Sphinx: The Character of Thomas Jefferson*. Among the most useful and succinct accounts of Williams's essential theology is W. Clark Gilpin's *The Millenarian Piety of Roger Williams*. See also James P. Byrd Jr., *The Challenges of Roger Williams: Religious Liberty, Violent Persecution, and the Bible* (the first chapter of which is entitled "The Modern Quest for the Elusive Roger Williams"), and James Calvin Davis, *The Moral Theology of Roger Williams: Christian Conviction and Public Ethics*, especially the chapters "Pluralism and Natural Morality" and "Conscience," 49–90.

5. Perry Miller, *Roger Williams: His Contribution to the American Tradition*, 55, 101; Myra Jehlen, *The Literature of Colonization*, 76. For a discussion of Miller's treatment of Williams as a thinker, see the Appendix.

6. *Complete Writings*, 1:359–60. This work is a reply to *A Letter of Mr. John Cottons, Teacher of the Church in Boston, in New England* (London, 1643), also printed in vol. 1 of *Complete Writings* (see 297–311) and quoted liberally by Williams in the course of his pamphlet.

7. John Eliot would seem to offer a similar case, but Eliot, in common with the much greater figure of Bartolomé de las Casas in New Spain a century earlier, acknowledges few if any uncertainties in his encounters with the Native Americans; they are subjects for conversion to an entirely orthodox Christianity and have little distinctive identity apart from this fact.

8. Among many instances, see *Complete Writings*, 1:390: "I humbly desire of the Father of Lights, that Mr. *Cotton*, and all that fear God may try what will abide the fiery trial in this *particular*, when the Lord Jesus shall be *revealed in flaming fire*, &c." Williams is praying that Cotton's conscience will be illuminated about the Bay Colonists' errors in regard to ministerial calling (an issue that Williams returns to several years later in *The Hireling Ministry None of Christs;* see *Complete Writings*, 7:149–91).

9. Ibid., 3:80–81, 55, 198 (I have reversed the italicization), 369.

10. Ibid., 3:275, 272, 208.

11. Ibid., 3:334. In her valuable discussion of *Key into the Language*'s poetry, Ivy Schweitzer places much emphasis on Williams's exile from Massachusetts Bay as the defining aspect of his authorial voice, enabling Williams to display a "flexible positional superiority," a phrase that Schweitzer borrows from Edward Said (see Schweitzer, *Work of Self-Representation*, 191). She argues that Williams's presentation of himself as an "other" to English and to Native Americans alike allows him to comment ironically on Puritan society without explicitly declaring allegiance to the "heathen" culture with which he is associated after 1635. (The influence of the new historicist paradigms of "self" and "other" are obvious throughout this reading.) My argument, on the other hand, turns on the idea that Williams is actually not much of an ironist, and that, as far as *Key into the Language* is con-

cerned, the "value" of exile lies in freeing up space for him to pursue lines of inquiry that would otherwise be inaccessible to him, at least in the local context of the Bay Colony.

12. *Complete Writings*, 3:180; Teunissen and Hinz, *Key into the Language*, 214 (I have reversed the italicization in the poem). I need say little here about the importance of gold in the colonial imagination, but I will note that the early English colonists were also interested in finding pearl fisheries in North America. Thomas Harriot, for instance, has a section on "Pearl" in the first part of *A Briefe and True Report*, in which he describes a crew member collecting roughly five thousand pearls from the local Native Americans, "of which number he chose so many as made a fair chain, which for their likeness and uniformity in roundness, orientness and piedness of many excellent colors, with equality in greatness, were very fair and rare" (*A Brief and True Report of the New Found Land of Virginia: The Complete 1590 Theodor de Bry Edition*, 11). Harriot claims that these pearls were lost on the return trip to England.

13. See both Schweitzer, *Work of Self-Representation* ("The parallel that Williams draws between these two groups [English and Native American], in contrast to himself, heightens the speaker's isolation and understated superiority" [185–86]), and Scanlan, *Colonial Writing* ("Rather than consisting of native inhabitants and English, the world that Williams attempts to describe is tripartite: native inhabitants, Massachusetts settlers, and himself" [133]).

14. Here, I use the terms of the passage from Garrett that I quoted earlier, and I follow lines of discussion from the work of John Canup and W. Clark Gilpin. See John Canup, *Out of the Wilderness: The Emergence of an American Identity in Colonial New England*, 133–48, and Gilpin, *Millenarian Piety*, 81–95. Gilpin points out that in using "witness" as a term, Williams always has in mind its Greek equivalent, *mártys*—Anglicized, of course, as "martyr" (81–82).

15. The comparison is in *A Reply to Mr. Williams his Examination*, included in the *Complete Writings* for its historical pertinence; see *Complete Writings*, 2:17. I am indebted to Canup for the reference; see *Out of the Wilderness*, 135.

16. *Complete Writings*, 3:186–87, 184; Teunissen and Hinz, *Key into the Language*, 175.

17. *Complete Writings*, 3:225, 105 (on this passage and the reasoning behind it, see also Byrd, *Challenges*, 114–16), 233, 242–43. Keith W. F. Stavely offers an interesting discussion of the garden trope, though with perhaps more emphasis on Williams's association with John Milton than the existing evidence will bear; see his "Roger Williams and the Enclosed Gardens of New England," esp. 261–64. See also Williams's "General Observations" to chapter 11, "Of Travel": "As the same Sun shines on the Wilderness that doth on a Garden! so the same faithful and all sufficient God, can comfort, feed and safely guide even through a desolate howling Wilderness" (Teunissen and Hinz, *Key into the Language*, 153).

18. *Complete Writings*, 3:320, 327, 328.

19. Schweitzer, *Work of Self-Representation*, 185, 212, has noted that Williams also occasionally employs a "Pauline" voice in *Key into the Language*.

20. *Complete Writings*, 3:95, 92, 159.

21. Ibid., 3:72–73, 250.

22. Jehlen, *Literature of Colonization*, 76; Schweitzer, *Work of Self-Representation*, 197; Anne G. Myles, "Dissent and the Frontier of Translation: Roger Williams's *A Key into the Language of America*," 106.

23. Teunissen and Hinz, *Key into the Language*, 30; Schweitzer, *Work of Self-Representation*, 188 (see also Myles, "Dissent," 107, where Williams's poetry is briefly compared to George Herbert's); Scanlan, *Colonial Writing*, 127. Teunissen and Hinz's introduction to their edition of *Key into the Language* represents the first sustained attempt to treat Williams as an artist. The authors conclude by admitting that the book is not a great "work of art," but they still see it as a formative element in the teleology of American literature, a teleology that culminates (as it has done so often) with the American Renaissance:

> in *A Key into the Language of America* are to be found some of the earliest expressions of qualities that have come to be regarded as characteristic of American literature, such as the self-reliance of an Emerson, the symbolic perspective of a Hawthorne, the tragic primitivism of a Melville, and the pragmatic empiricism of a Twain. In this sense, whereas most colonial writing must be described as literature written in or about America, Roger Williams's *Key* can be described as an early example of American literature. (69)

As a corrective to this rather whiggish assessment of *Key into the Language*, I want to suggest that there is still much to be learned by treating the work as an example of that lesser category "literature written in or about America."

24. In *The Bloudy Tenent*, Williams rarely shows much interest in the potential allegorical dimensions of his two interlocutors. For "Truth" one might as well substitute "Williams," and "Peace" could be replaced with "Williams's Interviewer" (who, of course, is none other than "Williams").

25. Teunissen and Hinz, *Key into the Language*, 83.

26. James Atkinson, "Forms of Dissent in the Puritan Sermon: William Perkins, John Cotton, and Roger Williams," 87.

27. Perry Miller, *The New England Mind: The Seventeenth Century*, 100. I am grateful to Martin Camargo for reminding me of the quantity of poetry in medieval didactic texts. In his research he has found a number of letter-writing (i.e., prose-writing) manuals of the period that are presented completely in verse; see Martin Camargo, "'Si dictare velis': Versified *Artes dictandi* and Late Medieval Writing Pedagogy."

28. *Complete Writings*, 7:18–19.

29. Ibid., 3:92.

30. Teunissen and Hinz, *Key into the Language,* 83–84. Schweitzer, *Work of Self Representation,* stresses the key as a symbol of power—the power, that is, of the gatekeeper, who can allow or prohibit entrance (192–93). Thus Williams is the "keeper of the key" and has an implicit advantage over those who lack it. However, the prestige of his position would seem to be lessened considerably by the fact that Williams plans to make and distribute multiple copies of this particular key. Perhaps it would be more precise to say this key is more a symbol of empowerment than of power.

31. Teunissen and Hinz, *Key into the Language,* 84. Williams is quite fond of this trope; see chapter 9 of *The Bloudy Tenent,* where he employs it negatively: Jesus "hath commanded his people to purge out the old leaven, not only greater portions, but a little leaven which will leaven the whole lump" (*Complete Writings,* 3:87). See also the negative example in chapter 101 (*Complete Writings,* 3:285).

32. Teunissen and Hinz, *Key into the Language,* 89. See also Williams's concluding remarks in ibid., 250.

33. Ibid., 84.

34. Ibid., 86, 85, 86–87.

35. Ibid., 86, 197.

36. This is perhaps close to what Rubertone has in mind when she calls *Key into the Language* "an instrument of discovery," though she does not develop the idea in much detail (*Grave Undertakings,* 96–97).

37. Myles, "Dissent," 98.

38. Teunissen and Hinz, *Key into the Language,* 88. See also the discussion of this passage in J. Patrick Cesarini, "The Ambivalent Uses of Roger Williams's *A Key into the Language of America,*" 475–77.

39. Teunissen and Hinz, *Key into the Language,* 135, 194, 195. Schweitzer, *Work of Self-Representation,* 215, offers a much more elaborate reading of the last passage, based on the notion that being "out of the way," thus lost, ironically applies to the Puritans as much as to the Native Americans. As to the association of phrases with particular speakers, Myles observes, "Perhaps most striking in these vocabulary passages is that it is frequently impossible to assign stable positions for Narragansetts or Englishmen. . . . In a sense, the very fragmentation of the dialogue forces the reader to recognize the universality of the role of the speaking subject" ("Dissent," 98).

40. Teunissen and Hinz, *Key into the Language,* 198–99. In the first passage the bracketed interpolation is mine; in the second passage, Teunissen and Hinz's. Pratt quotes this passage as one that "recognizes that meaning is not always apparent and there are multiple ways of gaining access to meaning with differing results." He concludes with a broader and more dubious claim: "Anticipating later pragmatists, Miantonomi appears to suggest that meaning is more than truth" (*Native Pragmatism,* 102, 103). But the episode is cryptic enough that its meaning can only be conjectural, and Pratt is rather too eager to fit Miantonomi

into his general argument that American pragmatism as a philosophical movement was influenced by the ideas and mores of Native American cultures.

41. Teunissen and Hinz, *Key into the Language,* 133, 113, 120. A New World–Old World comparison in a somewhat different register occurs in the gloss in chapter 11 on "Cuppì-machàug" *(Thick wood: a Swamp):* "These thick Woods and Swamps (like the Bogs to the *Irish*) are the Refuges for Women and children in War, whilst the men fight" (150). The Irish, of course, frequently figure as the Western European equivalent to Indians in sixteenth- and seventeenth-century colonial texts.

42. Ibid., 96, 134, 128, 170, 204, 208, 142, 145–46, 156. On death, see also 249: "O, how terrible is the look, the speedy and serious thought of death to all the sons of men?"

43. Ibid., 120. On the identity of the other tribe(s), James Hammond Trumbull's venerable Narragansett Club footnotes provide helpful guidance where Teunissen and Hinz are silent. Trumbull argues that both *Mihtukméchakick* and *Mauquaùog* are derogatory Eastern Algonquian terms for the Mohawk tribe. See *Complete Writings,* 1:102n31, 105n35.

44. Teunissen and Hinz, *Key into the Language,* 130. The first bracketed interpolation is mine; the second is Teunissen and Hinz's. Pratt quotes from this passage as well as the previous one (*Native Pragmatism,* 90, 90n19) in arguing that Williams's views drew upon the Narragansett custom of *wunnégin,* the extension of welcome and hospitality to strangers. Cannibals were the extreme version of such strangers in Native American (and, for that matter, European) society, yet Narragansett culture theoretically made a place for them at the feast—as they did for an English stranger such as Williams. Hence one of Pratt's chapters is entitled "Welcoming the Cannibals." See *Native Pragmatism,* 78–132.

45. Teunissen and Hinz, *Key into the Language,* 192; Myles, "Dissent," 90; Schweitzer, *Work of Self-Representation,* 228; Rubertone, *Grave Undertakings,* 97.

46. Schweitzer, *Work of Self-Representation,* 228.

47. For an extended critique, see Philip Gura, "The Study of Colonial American Literature, 1966–1987: A *Vade Mecum.*"

48. Teunissen and Hinz, *Key into the Language,* 194.

Conclusion: Chains of Knowledge

1. Gadamer, *Truth and Method,* 87.

Appendix: Perry Miller on Roger Williams

1. Miller, *Roger Williams,* 56. See also Sacvan Bercovitch, "Typology in Puritan New England: The Williams-Cotton Controversy Reassessed," and Thomas M. Davis, "The Traditions of Puritan Typology."

2. Miller, *Roger Williams*, 56; *Complete Writings* 7:12, 13, 14, 22, 23, 24.

3. *Complete Writings*, 7:161, 160, 183, 159.

4. This is a favorite verse of Williams; see, for instance, the eighth query in *Queries of Highest Consideration*, in *Complete Writings*, 2:27.

5. See Bercovitch, "Typology," 176–83.

6. Anne G. Myles, "Arguments in Milk, Arguments in Blood: Roger Williams, Persecution, and the Discourse of the Witness," 145.

7. For less dramatic but more balanced accounts of Williams's use of typology, see Edmund S. Morgan, *Roger Williams: The Church and the State*, Richard Reinitz, "The Separatist Background of Roger Williams' Argument for Religious Toleration," and Jesper Rosenmeier, "The Teacher and the Witness: John Cotton and Roger Williams." Byrd, *Challenges*, 31–48, provides a helpful summary of Miller's argument and the various critical responses to it.

Bibliography

—〰—

Adams, Charles Francis, Jr. *Three Episodes of Massachusetts History.* 5th ed., vol. 1. Boston, 1896.

Adams, Charles Francis, Jr., ed. *New English Canaan of Thomas Morton.* Prince Society Publications 14. 1883. Reprint, New York: Burt Franklin, 1967.

Anderson, Douglas. *William Bradford's Books: "Of Plimmoth Plantation" and the Printed Word.* Baltimore: Johns Hopkins University Press, 2003.

Arner, Robert D. "Pastoral Celebration and Satire in Thomas Morton's *New English Canaan.*" *Criticism* 16 (1974): 217–31.

Atkinson, James. "Forms of Dissent in the Puritan Sermon: William Perkins, John Cotton, and Roger Williams." Master's thesis, University of Missouri–Columbia, 1998.

Augustine. *The City of God against the Pagans.* Ed. and trans. R. W. Dyson. Cambridge: Cambridge University Press, 1998.

Axtell, James. *The European and the Indian: Essays in the Ethnohistory of North America.* Oxford: Oxford University Press, 1981.

Barber, C. L. *Shakespeare's Festive Comedy: A Study of Dramatic Form and Its Relation to Social Custom.* Princeton: Princeton University Press, 1959.

Barbour, Philip L., ed. *The Complete Works of Captain John Smith, 1580–1631.* 3 vols. Chapel Hill: University of North Carolina Press, 1986.

Barnaby, Andrew, and Lisa J. Schnell. *Literate Experience: The Work of Knowing in Seventeenth-Century English Writing.* New York: Palgrave, 2002.

Bercovitch, Sacvan. "Typology in Puritan New England: The Williams-Cotton Controversy Reassessed." *American Quarterly* 19 (1967): 166–91.

Bercovitch, Sacvan, ed. *The American Puritan Imagination: Essays in Revaluation.* Cambridge: Cambridge University Press, 1974.

———. *Typology and American Literature.* Amherst: University of Massachusetts Press, 1972.

Bercovitch, Sacvan, and Cyrus R. K. Patell, eds. *The Cambridge History of American Literature.* Vol. 1. Cambridge: Cambridge University Press, 1994.

Boehrer, Bruce. "Horatian Satire in Jonson's 'On the Famous Voyage.'" *Criticism* 44 (2002): 9–26.

Boelhower, William. "Mapping the Gift Path: Exchange and Rivalry in John Smith's 'A True Relation.'" *American Literary History* 15 (2003): 655–82.

Bradford, William. *Bradford's History "Of Plimoth Plantation."* Boston: [Commonwealth of Massachusetts], 1898.

―――. *History of Plymouth Plantation.* Ed. Massachusetts Historical Society. Boston: Houghton, 1912.

Bremer, Francis J. *Puritanism: Transatlantic Perspectives on a Seventeenth-Century Anglo-American Faith.* Boston: Massachusetts Historical Society, 1993.

Burckhardt, Jacob. *The Civilization of the Renaissance in Italy.* Trans. S. G. C. Middlemore; intro. Hajo Holborn. New York: Modern Library, 1954.

Burnham, Michelle. "Merchants, Money, and the Economics of 'Plain Style' in William Bradford's *Of Plymouth Plantation.*" *American Literature* 72 (2000): 695–720.

Byrd, James P., Jr. *The Challenges of Roger Williams: Religious Liberty, Violent Persecution, and the Bible.* Macon, Ga.: Mercer University Press, 2002.

Camargo, Martin. "'Si dictare velis': Versified *Artes dictandi* and Late Medieval Writing Pedagogy." *Rhetorica* 14 (1996): 265–88.

Canup, John. *Out of the Wilderness: The Emergence of an American Identity in Colonial New England.* Middletown, Conn.: Wesleyan University Press, 1990.

Carey, John, ed. *John Donne: A Critical Edition of the Major Works.* The Oxford Authors. Oxford: Oxford University Press, 1990.

Cartelli, Thomas. "Transplanting Disorder: The Construction of Misrule in Morton's *New English Canaan* and Bradford's *Of Plymouth Plantation.*" *English Literary Renaissance* 27 (1997): 258–80.

Cesarini, J. Patrick. "The Ambivalent Uses of Roger Williams's *A Key into the Language of America.*" *Early American Literature* 38 (2003): 469–94.

Cohen, Matt. "Morton's Maypole and the Indians: Publishing in Early New England." *Book History* 5 (2002): 1–18.

Collingwood, R. G. *The Idea of History.* Oxford: Clarendon Press, 1946.

Condon, Thomas J. *New York Beginnings: The Commercial Origins of New Netherland.* New York: New York University Press, 1968.

Connors, Donald F. *Thomas Morton.* New York: Twayne, 1969.

Conroy, David W. *In Public Houses: Drink and the Revolution of Authority in Colonial Massachusetts.* Chapel Hill: University of North Carolina Press, 1995.

Craven, Wesley Frank. *Dissolution of the Virginia Company: The Failure of a Colonial Experiment.* New York: Oxford University Press, 1932.

Cronon, William. *Changes in the Land: Indians, Colonists, and the Ecology of New England.* New York: Hill and Wang, 1983.

Daly, Robert. "William Bradford's Vision of History." *American Literature* 44 (1973): 557–69.

Davis, James Calvin. *The Moral Theology of Roger Williams: Christian Conviction and Public Ethics.* Louisville, Ky.: Westminster John Knox Press, 2004.

Davis, Thomas M. "The Traditions of Puritan Typology." In Bercovitch, *Typology,* 11–45.

Dempsey, Jack. "Reading the Revels: The Riddle of May Day in *New English Canaan*." *Early American Literature* 34 (1999): 283–312.

Dempsey, Jack, ed. *New English Canaan by Thomas Morton of "Merrymount": Text, Notes, Biography, and Criticism.* Scituate, Mass.: Digital Scanning, 2000.

Dexter, Henry Martin, and Morton Dexter. *The England and Holland of the Pilgrims.* 1906. Reprint, Baltimore: Genealogical Publishing, 1978.

Donegan, Kathleen. "'As Dying, yet Behold We Live': Catastrophe and Interiority in Bradford's *Of Plymouth Plantation*." *Early American Literature* 37 (2002): 9–37.

Elliott, Emory. *New England Puritan Literature.* In Bercovitch and Patell, *Cambridge History*, 171–306.

Elliott, J. H. "Final Reflections: The Old World and the New Revisited." In Kupperman, *America*, 391–408.

———. *The Old World and the New, 1492–1650.* Cambridge: Cambridge University Press, 1970.

Ellis, Joseph J. *American Sphinx: The Character of Thomas Jefferson.* New York: Knopf, 1997.

Emerson, Everett, ed. *Major Writers of Early American Literature.* Madison: University of Wisconsin Press, 1972.

Erickson, Peter, and Clark Hulse, eds. *Early Modern Visual Culture: Representation, Race, and Empire in Renaissance England.* Philadelphia: University of Pennsylvania Press, 2000.

Ferguson, Arthur B. *Clio Unbound: Perception of the Social and Cultural Past in Renaissance England.* Duke Monographs in Medieval and Renaissance Studies 2. Durham: Duke University Press, 1979.

Fitzmaurice, Andrew. *Humanism and America: An Intellectual History of English Colonisation, 1500–1625.* Cambridge: Cambridge University Press, 2003.

Frampton, John. *Joyfull Newes Out of the New Founde Worlde, Written in Spanish by Nicholas Monardes Physician of Seville and Englished by John Frampton, Merchant Anno 1577.* Vol. 1. Intro. Stephen Gaselee. The Tudor Translations 2d ser., 9. Gen. ed. Charles Whibley. London: Constable, 1925.

Franklin, Wayne. *Discoverers, Explorers, Settlers: The Diligent Writers of Early America.* Chicago: University of Chicago Press, 1979.

Fuller, Mary C. *Voyages in Print: English Travel to America, 1576–1624.* Cambridge: Cambridge University Press, 1995.

Gadamer, Hans-Georg. *Truth and Method.* Trans. Garrett Barden and John Cumming. New York: Seabury-Continuum, 1975.

Garrett, John. *Roger Williams: Witness beyond Christendom, 1603–1683.* London: Macmillan, 1970.

Gilpin, W. Clark. *The Millenarian Piety of Roger Williams.* Chicago: University of Chicago Press, 1979.

Greenblatt, Stephen. *Renaissance Self-Fashioning: From More to Shakespeare.* Chicago: University of Chicago Press, 1980.

————. *Shakespearean Negotiations: The Circulation of Social Energy in Renaissance England.* Berkeley and Los Angeles: University of California Press, 1988.

Greenblatt, Stephen, ed. *New World Encounters.* Berkeley: University of California Press, 1993.

Griffith, John. *"Of Plymouth Plantation* as a Mercantile Epic." *Arizona Quarterly* 28 (1972): 231–42.

Gura, Philip. "The Study of Colonial American Literature, 1966–1987: A *Vade Mecum.*" *William and Mary Quarterly,* 3d ser., 45 (1988): 305–41.

Gustafson, Sandra M. *Eloquence Is Power: Oratory and Performance in Early America.* Chapel Hill: University of North Carolina Press, 2000.

Haller, William. *The Rise of Puritanism; or, The Way to the New Jerusalem as Set Forth in Pulpit and Press from Thomas Cartwright to John Lilburne and John Milton, 1570–1643.* 1938. Reprint, New York: Harper Torchbooks, 1957.

Harriot, Thomas. *A Briefe and True Report of the New Found Land of Virginia: The Complete 1590 Theodor de Bry Edition.* Intro. Paul Hulton. New York: Dover, 1972.

Helgerson, Richard. *Forms of Nationhood: The Elizabethan Writing of England.* Chicago: University of Chicago Press, 1992.

Herford, C. H., and Percy Simpson, eds. *Ben Jonson.* Oxford: Clarendon, 1925–1952. Vols. 1, 2 (1925), 8 (1947).

Hoffer, Peter Charles. *Sensory Worlds in Early America.* Baltimore: Johns Hopkins University Press, 2003.

Holquist, Michael, ed. *The Dialogic Imagination: Four Essays by M. M. Bakhtin.* Trans. Caryl Emerson and Michael Holquist. Austin: University of Texas Press, 1981.

Hovey, Kenneth Alan. "The Theology of History in *Of Plymouth Plantation* and Its Predecessors." *Early American Literature* 10 (1975): 47–66.

Howard, Alan B. "Art and History in Bradford's *Of Plymouth Plantation.*" *William and Mary Quarterly,* 3d ser., 28 (1971): 237–66.

Howard, Jean E., and Scott Cutler Shershow, eds. *Marxist Shakespeares.* London: Routledge, 2001.

Hulme, Peter. *Colonial Encounters: Europe and the Native Caribbean, 1492–1797.* London: Methuen, 1986.

————. "Making No Bones: A Response to Myra Jehlen." *Critical Inquiry* 20 (1993): 179–86.

Jameson, J. Franklin, ed. *Johnson's Wonder-Working Providence, 1628–1651.* New York: Scribner, 1910.

Jehlen, Myra. "History before the Fact; or, Captain John Smith's Unfinished Symphony." *Critical Inquiry* 19 (1993): 677–92.

————. *The Literature of Colonization.* In Bercovitch and Patell, *Cambridge History,* 13–168.

————. "Response to Peter Hulme." *Critical Inquiry* 20 (1993): 187–91.

Johnson, Richard R. "The Search for a Usable Indian: An Aspect of the Defense of Colonial New England." *Journal of American History* 64 (1977): 623–51.

Kammen, Michael. *Colonial New York: A History.* New York: Scribner, 1975.

Knapp, Jeffrey. *An Empire Nowhere: England, America, and Literature from "Utopia" to "The Tempest."* Berkeley and Los Angeles: University of California Press, 1992.

Kupperman, Karen Ordahl. *Indians and English: Facing Off in Early America.* Ithaca: Cornell University Press, 2000.

———. "Thomas Morton, Historian." *New England Quarterly* 50 (1977): 660–64.

Kupperman, Karen Ordahl, ed. *America in European Consciousness, 1493–1750.* Chapel Hill: University of North Carolina Press, 1995.

———. *Captain John Smith: A Select Edition of His Writings.* Chapel Hill: University of North Carolina Press, 1988.

Laurence, David. "William Bradford's American Sublime." *PMLA* 102 (1987): 55–65.

Lechford, Thomas. *Plain Dealing; or, News from New England.* Ed. J. Hammond Trumbull. 1867. Reprint, New York: Garrett, 1970.

Levin, David. "William Bradford: The Value of Puritan Historiography." In Emerson, *Major Writers,* 11–31.

Lévi-Strauss, Claude. *The Savage Mind.* Chicago: University of Chicago Press, 1966.

Levy, F. J. *Tudor Historical Thought.* San Marino, Calif.: Huntington Library, 1967.

McLeod, Bruce. *The Geography of Empire in English Literature, 1580–1745.* Cambridge: Cambridge University Press, 1999.

McRae, Andrew. "'On the Famous Voyage': Ben Jonson and Civic Space." *Early Modern Literary Studies,* special issue 3, no. 8 (1998): 1–31. http://purl.oclc.org/emls/04–2/macraonth.htm.

McWilliams, John. *New England's Crises and Cultural Memory: Literature, Politics, History, Religion, 1620–1860.* Cambridge Studies in American Literature and Culture 142. Cambridge: Cambridge University Press, 2004.

Meinig, D. W. *The Shaping of America: A Geographical Perspective on 500 Years of History.* New Haven: Yale University Press, 1986.

Miller, Perry. *Errand into the Wilderness.* Cambridge: Harvard University Press, 1956.

———. *The New England Mind: The Seventeenth Century.* Cambridge: Harvard University Press, 1939.

———. "Roger Williams: An Essay in Interpretation." In Williams, *Complete Writings,* 7:5–25.

———. *Roger Williams: His Contribution to the American Tradition.* Indianapolis: Bobbs-Merrill, 1953.

Mitchell, W. J. T., ed. *On Narrative.* Chicago: University of Chicago Press, 1981.

Montaigne, Michel de. *The Essays: A Selection.* Trans. and ed. M. A. Screech. Harmondsworth, England: Penguin, 1993.

Morgan, Edmund S. *American Slavery, American Freedom: The Ordeal of Colonial Virginia*. New York: Norton, 1975.

———. *Roger Williams: The Church and the State*. New York: Harcourt, 1967.

Morison, Samuel Eliot, ed. *Of Plymouth Plantation, 1620–1647, by William Bradford Sometime Governor Thereof*. New York: Knopf, 1952.

Mullaney, Steven. "Imaginary Conquests: European Material Technologies and the Colonial Mirror Stage." In Erickson and Hulse, *Visual Culture*, 15–43.

Myles, Anne G. "Arguments in Milk, Arguments in Blood: Roger Williams, Persecution, and the Discourse of the Witness." *Modern Philology* 91 (1993): 133–60.

———. "Dissent and the Frontier of Translation: Roger Williams's *A Key into the Language of America*." In St. George, *Possible Pasts*, 88–108.

Nash, Gary B. "The Image of the Indian in the Southern Colonial Mind." *William and Mary Quarterly*, 3d ser., 29 (1972): 197–230.

O'Gorman, Edmundo. *The Invention of America: An Inquiry into the Historical Nature of the New World and the Meaning of Its History*. Bloomington: Indiana University Press, 1961.

Poovey, Mary. *A History of the Modern Fact: Problems of Knowledge in the Sciences of Wealth and Society*. Chicago: University of Chicago Press, 1998.

Pratt, Scott L. *Native Pragmatism: Rethinking the Roots of American Philosophy*. Bloomington: Indiana University Press, 2002.

Prest, Wilfrid R. *The Inns of Court under Elizabeth I and the Early Stuarts, 1590–1640*. London: Longman, 1972.

Quint, David. *Epic and Empire: Politics and Generic Form from Virgil to Milton*. Princeton: Princeton University Press, 1993.

Ralegh, Sir Walter. *The Discoverie of the Large, Rich and Bewtiful Empyre of Guiana*. Ed. V. T. Harlow. London: Argonaut, 1928.

Reinitz, Richard. "The Separatist Background of Roger Williams' Argument for Religious Toleration." In Bercovitch, *Typology*, 107–37.

Rider, Clare. "Lost in the Past: The Rediscovered Archives of Clifford's Inn." *Inner Temple Yearbook*, 1998–1999. http://www.innertemple.org.uk/history/clifford.html.

Riggs, David. *Ben Jonson: A Life*. Cambridge: Harvard University Press, 1989.

Rosenmeier, Jesper. "The Teacher and the Witness: John Cotton and Roger Williams." *William and Mary Quarterly*, 3d ser., 25 (1968): 408–31.

———. "'With My Owne Eyes': William Bradford's *Of Plymouth Plantation*." In Bercovitch, *Puritan Imagination*, 77–106.

Rossiter, A. P. *Angel with Horns and Other Shakespeare Lectures*. Ed. Graham Storey. New York: Theatre Arts, 1961.

Rubertone, Patricia E. *Grave Undertakings: An Archaeology of Roger Williams and the Narragansett Indians*. Washington, D.C.: Smithsonian Institution Press, 2001.

Rutman, Darrett B. *Winthrop's Boston: Portrait of a Puritan Town, 1630–1649*. Chapel Hill: University of North Carolina Press, 1965.

Sargent, Mark L. "William Bradford's 'Dialogue' with History." *New England Quarterly* 65 (1992): 389–421.

Sargent, Ralph M. *At the Court of Queen Elizabeth: The Life and Lyrics of Sir Edward Dyer.* London: Oxford University Press, 1935.

Scanlan, Thomas. *Colonial Writing and the New World, 1583–1671: Allegories of Desire.* Cambridge: Cambridge University Press, 1999.

Schweitzer, Ivy. *The Work of Self-Representation: Lyric Poetry in Colonial New England.* Chapel Hill: University of North Carolina Press, 1991.

Seelye, John. *Prophetic Waters: The River in Early American Life and Literature.* New York: Oxford University Press, 1977.

Shea, Daniel. "'Our Professed Old Adversary': Thomas Morton and the Naming of New England." *Early American Literature* 23 (1988): 52–69.

Smith, Bruce R. "Mouthpieces: Native American Voices in Thomas Harriot's *A True and Brief Report of . . . Virginia* [sic], Gaspar Pérez de Villagrá's *Historia de la Nuevo México,* and John Smith's *General History of Virginia.*" *New Literary History* 32 (2001): 501–17.

Stavely, Keith W. F. "Roger Williams and the Enclosed Gardens of New England." In Bremer, *Puritanism,* 257–74.

Stechow, Wolfgang. *Dutch Landscape Painting of the Seventeenth Century.* London: Phaidon, 1966.

St. George, Robert Blair, ed. *Possible Pasts: Becoming Colonial in Early America.* Ithaca: Cornell University Press, 2000.

Taylor, E. G. R., ed. *The Original Writings and Correspondence of the Two Richard Hakluyts.* 2 vols. Hakluyt Society, 2d ser., 76–77. London: Hakluyt Society, 1935.

Teunissen, John J., and Evelyn J. Hinz, eds. *A Key into the Language of America,* by Roger Williams. Detroit: Wayne State University Press, 1973.

Todorov, Tzvetan. *The Conquest of America: The Question of the Other.* Trans. Richard Howard. New York: Harper, 1984.

Usher, Roland Greene. "Allerton, Isaac." *Dictionary of American Biography.* 1964 edition.

Vickers, Brian, ed. *Francis Bacon.* Oxford Authors. Oxford: Oxford University Press, 1996.

Walsh, W. H. *Philosophy of History: An Introduction.* Rev. ed. New York: Torchbooks-Harper, 1967.

Warner, Michael. "What's Colonial about Colonial America?" In St. George, *Possible Pasts,* 49–70.

Wenska, Walter P. "Bradford's Two Histories: Pattern and Paradigm in *Of Plymouth Plantation.*" *Early American Literature* 13 (1978): 151–64.

White, Hayden. "The Historical Text as Literary Artifact." *Clio: An Interdisciplinary Journal of Literature, History, and the Philosophy of History* 3 (1974): 277–303.

———. *Metahistory: The Historical Imagination in Nineteenth-Century Europe.* Baltimore: Johns Hopkins University Press, 1973.

———. "The Value of Narrativity in the Representation of Reality." In Mitchell, *On Narrative*, 1–23.

Williams, Roger. *The Complete Writings of Roger Williams.* 7 vols. New York: Russell and Russell, 1963.

Williamson, Margaret Holmes. *Powhatan Lords of Life and Death: Command and Consent in Seventeenth-Century Virginia.* Lincoln: University of Nebraska Press, 2003.

Winthrop, John. *Winthrop Papers.* Vol. 2. Boston: Massachusetts Historical Society, 1931.

Wood, William. *New England's Prospect.* Ed. Alden T. Vaughan. Amherst: University of Massachusetts Press, 1977.

Zuckerman, Michael. "Pilgrims in the Wilderness: Community, Modernity, and the Maypole at Merry Mount." *New England Quarterly* 50 (1977): 255–77.

Index

—ᴍ—